Author of

No-Nonsense Life Skills: Managing Your Stress

Picking Up the Pieces: Moving On After a Significant Loss

Growing Through Life: When Snorkeling Jello Just Doesn't Cut It

Healing the Broken Heart

A Beacon of Hope for the Bereaved

James Ray Ashurst, Ph. D.

WESTBOW
P R E S S®
A DIVISION OF THOMAS NELSON
& ZONDERVAN

Scripture references from The Scofield Reference Bible, Copyright © 1909, 1917; copyright renewed 1937, 1945 by Oxford university Press, Inc

WestBow Press books may be ordered through booksellers or by contacting:

WestBow Press
A Division of Thomas Nelson & Zondervan
1663 Liberty Drive
Bloomington, IN 47403
www.westbowpress.com
1 (866) 928-1240

ISBN: 978-1-9736-3461-4 (sc)
ISBN: 978-1-9736-3460-7 (hc)
ISBN: 978-1-9736-3462-1 (e)

Library of Congress Control Number: 2018908448

Print information available on the last page.

WestBow Press rev. date: 07/24/2018

*How we walk with the broken speaks louder
than how we sit with the great.*
—Tobymac

This book is dedicated to all those who call me "Friend"

Contents

Acknowledgments

I am indebted to these three ladies who gave up their time to proofread this manuscript:

Carolyn Baker
Jackie Frakes
Sandy Slee

The phenomenal cover of this book was created by a genius of photography, Chris Hefferen.

If you were drawn to the cover, the credit entirely belongs to him.

Introduction

The deaths of both my parents were unexpected, and thus, a tremendous shock in my life. My seemingly perfect life came to a piercing, screeching, gut-wrenching halt. Life, as I knew it, was no longer copasetic. It was far from it. Temporarily, it became a world of confusion, unbelief, and horrific sadness.

To me at the time, it seemed as if the world was spinning out of control, and I was in the midst of the chaos. My rational thinking was labored, and I was on an emotional roller coaster—a scary and unsure ride.

My loving mother was the first to succumb to death, and then just a few years later, unwelcomed death knocked loudly and snatched my wonderful father. On that dreadful day, my brother and I became adult orphans.

Of the two deaths, the unique one was that of my mom. An extraordinary experience and eye-opening life lesson took place for me after the funeral service, on the way to the grave site service.

Rationally, I knew that "life" didn't stop for others just because one had suffered the death of a loved one. I knew it in my alert mind. It's the emotions that didn't coincide with the mentality.

On the way to my mother's grave site, traffic was as normal as it usually was on any ordinary day. People had errands to do or appointments to keep. Traffic was congested.

Being in a funeral procession, vehicles in all directions stopped to give us priority. The individuals were demonstrating the utmost respect. Once we had passed, the cars sped on their way to various destinations.

One would have assumed that I would have been pleased, but I wasn't. At that moment, I was far from it.

Sitting in the car, I wanted a complete halt of everyone who was walking by and every vehicle that had begun to move to come to a standstill. *"Did those people not know who was being buried?"* *"Did they not comprehend what I was enduring?"* *"How dare they get on with life?"*

Furthermore, I was actually becoming angry. No longer was I focusing on the horrible death of my beloved mother but rather on the supposed "insensitivity" of the nearby population.

What brought me out of my irrational self-absorption was a complete stranger in a sheriff uniform. While still perturbed, I gazed out the car window and saw the gentleman, directing traffic. As our procession passed by, he removed his hat and held it tightly to his chest—a loving respect for my mom.

The idea of never hearing my mother's voice of pure sweetness, like honey, was overwhelmingly traumatic for me. Just a month before, when I was with her, she looked frail but certainly not a welcomed visitor at the threshold of death.

What God does is not always immediately evident to human eyes.
—John Claypool

And then several years later, my dad followed. Still another voice that would never reverberate in sentences or songs. His deep voice resonated on a perfect pitch level. His base voice was melodious.

Being an adult orphan can be difficult to absorb into one's thinking processes-- a strange awareness of being left all alone to maneuver life without one's mighty heroes. The mind becomes confused and twisted as to the absenteeism of those who once were, the emotions hit painfully hard like waves against the mighty cliffs, and the physical still longs to see one more glimpse of the missing persons.

No thoughtful sentiments or benevolent actions or sentimental gestures can even approach the hem of the garment of comfort. I felt an excruciating loss, mixed with a horrific sadness of the highest intensity that reaches the very depths of a person's soul that seems at the time inconsolable.

Individuals who have experienced similar grief-stricken events can readily identify the bombardment of raw grief and are not the same person as before. The death of a significant family member, young or elderly, changes the dynamics of the entire family system and involves each and every family individual.

The most intriguing mystery that has perplexed the very essence of mankind is the swirling dynamics surrounding death and its aftermath. Theologians have expounded on an assortment of the varied possibilities of spirituality, philosophers have issued forth thought-provoking proposals, worthy scholars have submitted years of their long-suffering days of their diligent research to interpret centuries of scripture regarding death, and the curiosity of the "man on the street" has tried to conjure up some reasonable amount of elucidation that can satisfy one's ever-persisting curiosity.

Simply speaking, many years ago, it had to jolt family members and friends when the very first "Death" took place. At the time, humans did not know such a phenomenon could occur. At that moment in time, a specific person was taking in oxygen for sustainable breathing, exhaling out the colorless and odorless carbon dioxide in order to successfully complete the cycle of life, and then quite inexplicably, Boom! the individual became part of an unexplainable form of no communication—Death.

Survivor—a person who has survived an ordeal or great misfortune.
—Webster's New World College Dictionary

1

Death and the Parkers

It was a quiet evening. A soft snowfall covered the ground, and no one was seen on the streets because of the frigid temperatures. The Christmas holidays had finally begun. Beautiful decorations made neighborhoods look festive, and Christmas trees, outside and inside of the homes, paved the way for a joyous celebration of the season.

However, when the doorbell chimed unexpectedly at 108 Chestnut Street, the world of the Parkers changed instantly and forever. When Mrs. Parker opened the door, an army officer and an army chaplain were standing at attention, with faces of regret and sadness. The joyous celebrations, that the neighbors of the Parkers were experiencing, fell flat and empty in the living room of Mom and Dad Parker on that cold, snowy December night.

Their son, Joey, had wanted to be in the military since arriving at adolescence. He wanted to serve his beloved country, and carefully planned out his strategy. He knew what requirements had to be met before he enlisted, and his goal in life became cemented.

To prepare himself physically, Joey started his high school career by joining the wrestling team. He learned the techniques from his coach, becoming quite skilled in the sport. Due to his muscular prowess, he was sought after by the football and track coaches. They had been watching his energy level, his power of focus and concentration, and his strong determination to learn, so he became "scouted" by the other coaches.

Joey saw that these sports would be his answer to becoming military "fit" and mentally prepared for that date of enlistment. He would often compare himself to a tiger, ready for conquering and for surviving.

While his parents never discouraged him from his life goal, they also did not eagerly promote it. His parents would have lots of concerning conversations about their only child and his dream.

Mrs. Parker hoped dearly that her son would eventually change his direction, and often times in conversations suggested to him other careers that were "out there" to consider. Out of loving respect for his mom he promised to think about them, but deep, deep inside, Joey knew the direction in which he was heading.

Joey progressed through his high school classes in fine style, making good marks. His teachers loved the manner in which he approached his studies. With diligent concentration, stern focus, and keen perspicacity, Joey was "the student" that all the teachers wanted in their classes.

His popularity with his classmates earned him various roles in extracurricular clubs: Key Club President, Student Government President, and associate editor of the school newspaper. Joey was learning "the ropes" of being a distinguished leader. His accomplishments throughout high school were so many that one would honestly think that he didn't have time to attend classes too. In short, Joey was a huge success story.

Mom and Dad Parker knew instinctively the reason for the unscheduled visit from the military personnel. The conversation was cordial at first. The military officer was to be conducting the communication, but for whatever the reason, he was hesitating. The Parkers watched him take a deep breath: *"Mr. and Mrs. Parker, I have sad news about your son."*

In Joey's senior year, he had fallen in love with Sara who was also a senior. Sara was not only gorgeous but also had a sparkling personality. She made "heads" turn with no effort. She was madly in love with Joey. Her soft spoken voice whispered to Joey over and over again of her gentle love and commitment. In response, Joey would always smile widely and squeeze gently the hand of his beloved Sara. Their love grew deeply, convinced that God had brought them together as "one"--an unconditional love.

As Joey approached his graduation, his spirit over enlisting grew intensely. He had reached his eighteenth birthday, and by society, he was considered to be an adult. But not by his mom. He would always be her "baby" and was reminded of such continuously by her. She had ended all conversations regarding his enlisting in the military. With quiet thoughts and anxious feelings, she resigned herself to what Joey planned to do after graduation.

The month of September came; Joey enlisted. His mom and dad and Sara were on hand at the swearing-in ritual. Joey's departure date for military training was scheduled for October, and it came quickly. "Putting" Joey on the plane that day was one of the toughest actions that Mrs. Parker had ever done. With fake smiles, Sara and the Parkers waved goody-bye. Whenever Joey could, he would return for visits. With every visit, it became harder and harder to place Joey on the plane. Joey was well aware of the fake smiles, and eventually he saw in his parents' eyes the hurt, the worry, and the anxiety.

In the living room of the Parkers, there came a sharp chill that seemed to beat the chill of outdoors.

"Your son was killed by mortar fire on his unit. He didn't suffer. He was a superb military soldier. I am so sorry. What can we do for you? Make any phone calls?"

The air was sucked out of the room. Mr. Parker escorted the officer and the chaplain to the front door.

When he returned to the living room, his wife was staring out the bay window. When she heard him in the room, she turned slowly towards him. They embraced tightly, their shoulders began to shake uncontrollably, and they wept long into the night.

When Joey got his military assignment to be stationed in Afghanistan, he was both sad and happy, if such were possible: sad to be leaving his parents, of course, and Sara, but happy to finally be a "real bona fide" military person. On the day of his departure, one could cut the tension and sadness with a dull knife.

Dad and Mom Parker had an uncharacteristic look of grief and despair while Sara's countenance registered sorrow and helplessness. Joey's departure was felt for hours long after the plane had departed from the airport.

The specific Afghanistan assignment was to be simple: 15 minutes in the situation, then immediate departure. But it didn't go as planned. Fifteen minutes in...no departure...never again to be seen alive.

"It just wasn't supposed to happen!" cried out the Sergeant. The burly sergeant dropped helplessly to the desert ground, crying into his worn-out hands, as he surveyed three of the four team members lying dead, including the youngest one of all, Joey.

The Parkers were notified that Joey's body would be accessible at Atlanta Hartsfield-Jackson Airport on January 28 at approximately 3:30 P.M. A date and time that would forever more be planted and revered in the minds of the Parkers.

On January 28, Joey's parents with his beloved Sara, were awaiting anxiously on the tarmac to welcome home their son's body. It was a cool day in Atlanta, with temperatures in the mid-50s. The sun was in hiding, and the day could be described as extremely gloomy with an ever so light wind blowing.

The "death plane" arrived at 3:40. Military personnel stood at attention—rigid. The Parkers and Sara followed such protocol. The sight of the unwelcomed casket, with the glorious American flag draping it in military fashion, startled them. They were simply not ready or prepared for the forthcoming ceremony.

The casket was secured and handled with tenderness and professional care by those in uniform. No words were spoken. Facial expressions were solid and still.

Mom Parker had truly desired to maintain her composure—fully in control of herself. But a mom's intrinsic nature was in full operation, and at the sight of the casket carrying her son's body, Mrs. Parker of 108 Chestnut Street fell emotionally apart. The tears flowed, her shoulders responded violently, and her murmuring was subdued with tones of raw agony and sadness.

Mr. Parker forced down his emotional devastation in order to help his wife with her grieving reactions. Sara's beautiful countenance was clouded by tears, and plenty of them. For some unexplainable reason, Sara turned around and gazed upwards. What she saw stole away her breath. Returning her glance was what looked like dozens of spectators staring at the drama on the tarmac.

The curious individuals were inside the Atlanta airport, waiting patiently to catch their flights. Sara witnessed so many things that touched her already broken heart: Gentlemen were taking off their hats out of genuine respect. Ladies were removing handkerchiefs to wipe away their tears. Boys were offering military salutes. And girls seemed to be crying softly onto the quivering shoulders of their moms. For Sara at that precise moment, time seemed to stand absolutely frozen.

Life at 108 Chestnut Street was dormant for the remaining years that housed the Parkers. The sparkle disappeared, the glow dissipated, the kindness turned into gloominess, life became mundane ...and Joey became no more.

⟨⟩

The life of the dead is placed in the memory of the living.
—Marcus Cicero

⟨⟩

2

What Not to Say

When we are trying to show support to the bereaved through our words, we sometimes say things that can be misunderstood or even hurtful. The following is a list of taboo sentiments that should be avoided if at all possible.

"It's for the best."

This sentiment may be true if the loved one is suffering due to a terminal illness. We do not want to see our loved one in misery, pain, and torment. We might even subconsciously want to see our loved one take that final breath. We certainly do not vocalize such a wish, but the thought may be there.

However, when we are trying to say something comforting to the survivor, we may make things worse when we express that the death was somewhat ideal.

Even if the survivors agree consciously, they are not prepared to acknowledge the sentiment. They are in the process of accepting the death of their loved one, and they aren't ready to hear that the death was a good thing. We need to put ourselves in the shoes of the survivors as best we can. Maybe the death was best, but the survivors do not need to be reminded of such.

A suggestion of sentiment: *"I know you are hurting, and I'm right here for you."*

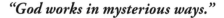

"God works in mysterious ways."

It is absolutely correct that God works in mysterious ways from our human standpoint. As humans, we cannot "touch the hem of the garment" when trying to figure out why God is doing or allowing certain events or things to happen. We are not on the same level of God: never have been and never will be.

When a survivor hears this sentiment, he or she tries to understand why God has allowed their beloved to die. The death may have been a child, a teenager, or an adult in the prime of life. The survivors may wonder if only they had been closer to God, the death would not have occurred.

Another concern on the part of the survivors is accepting the mystery of God. They may feel as "victims" of God and that if they aren't perfect, then God's mysterious self will be enacted by claiming the life of the beloved.

The truth about God's mysterious ways is simply that we are not privy to the Sovereign acts of God.

"Eventually you'll get over it."

A survivor is not ready to hear or acknowledge such a sentiment. It may be true that in time, the individual will learn to accept the death of a loved one. However, when the pain is still present, the survivor does not need to try to "escape the Pain" and immediately go to acceptance. Feelings and thoughts need to be expressed and to be dealt with. The grieving process takes time which must be respected and honored by the supportive individuals. The grieving process has specific levels which must be accomplished before the acceptance of the death is reached. The levels are the following: (1) Denial, shock. (2) Anger. (3) Depression. (4) Guilt. (5) Acceptance.

While levels #2-#4 may be in a different order, the bereaved must deal with all the levels to reach #5—acceptance.

A suggestion for a sentiment:

> **"I know you need to go through the grieving process, and I'll be by your side while you do."**

> **It is not death that a man should fear, but he should fear never beginning to live.**
> —Marcus Aurelius

> **"You'll get to see your loved one again one day."**

The bereaved may believe the sentiment, but during the time of the excruciating pain, the bereaved does not want to wait to see the loved one again. The survivor wants to see the loved one NOW. No waiting. No hoping. No anticipation. "NOW" is the "magic" word for the bereaved. Not in the future but right now. Perhaps the bereaved had positive things to say to the loved one or places to go together. The bereaved wants to have the loved one in the present—here and now—and in the future.

The supportive individuals need to allow such feelings of the bereaved. If only just for an hour, the bereaved may wish for the loved one to be with them. Such a feeling is normal, and friends should not negate the wishes of the bereaved. Friends and family members need to be available to the bereaved in the capacity of supporting the feelings and thoughts of the survivors. It is not the responsibility of the supportive individuals to judge or analyze the bereaved. Being accessible during the person's grieving process and afterwords is the role of the supportive friends and relatives.

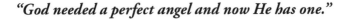

"God needed a perfect angel and now He has one."

God does not need perfect angels in Heaven. He already has angelic angels. The problem with this sentiment is that if God needed a perfect angel, why didn't He select someone else's child rather than the one He did? This attitude sounds like it is sacrilegious on the part of the bereaved. However, considering the ongoing pain, it is quite understandable for the bereaved to feel as such. The bereaved needs to have the freedom to express such thoughts without condemnation from anyone.

Emotional pain is far worse than a physical one. Due to modern medicine, physical pain can be dealt with successfully. However, when emotional pain is present, there is no medicine to get rid of the deep pain and hurt. The pain cuts deep. It can immobilize a person. Relief is not available at times. Therefore, when the bereaved is vocalizing feelings that seem sacrilegious, it is the emotional pain and hurt that is talking. The bereaved had to witness the death of their "angelic" child, and it is irrational to think the bereaved should be rational.

"Something better will come along."

In the minds of the survivors, this sentiment is most difficult to hear and to fully believe. There is no "better" with a person who has to deal with the recent death of a precious loved one. In his or her mind and emotions, the world of the bereaved is chaotic, totally unsettling, and hopeless. They have had to say good-bye to an important individual, to select an appropriate casket, to deal with well-meaning visitors, to endure a funeral, and to be at a grave site of farewells.

In reality, of course, something better will come along. Anything has to be better than dealing with the demise of a loved one. At the time, however, nothing can get worse or better. One's life is altered forever because a valuable and precious person has left a void. Such a void can never be filled. No one or no thing can fill the empty chair at the table.

Life does move forward, and it will inevitably become better. However, during the mourning period of time, the survivor may not accept that normal life is going to return in some shape and form.

A suggestion of a sentiment can be the following:

> *"There will be a future day when the pain will lessen, and life will return, I promise."*

> *"You need to pull yourself up by the bootstraps and get on with life."*

This is one of the most "unfeeling" comments that can be offered to a grieving individual. This is a premature statement because each person grieves differently and at his or her timetable. The survivor may not be prepared to "get on with life" and he or she should never be rushed to recovery.

This sentiment is loaded with guilt. The survivors may believe that they are spending too much time grieving over a loved one. As a result, they can feel guilty.

Individuals have the personal right to work at one's own pace when traveling through the mourning process. These individuals will know instinctively when it is time to "pick oneself up by the bootstraps" and move forward.

A suggestion of sentiment:

> *"When you are ready, I'll be available for you to go wherever you wish."*

> *"May your loved one rest in peace."*

This sentiment has no true meaning. It is a cliché that has been said over and over at grave sites for years. And thus, it is still used.

The shell of the deceased lies in the casket, but not the person's spirit/soul. When the last breath is taken, the spirit leaves the physical body and becomes an entity unto itself.

When I hear this sentiment, I wonder what the person is really meaning. Are we asking that the deceased body live in peace or the spirit/soul? I must assume it means the person's spirit. If that is true, then the assumption is that the spirit is what people mean when they use this sentiment.

One has to wonder why wouldn't the person's soul/spirit be at peace? For a Christian, it has no more worries or conflicts. It is in eternity. Peace is already at work once the spirit leaves the physical body.

The bereaved does not need the extra burden of wondering if their loved one is at peace. The survivors need to hear a positive affirmation that yes! your loved one is finally at peace, having left the physical self.

"She is in a better place."

While the survivor may mentally own the idea that the loved one is in a better place, the emotions do not necessarily agree. The survivor is grief-stricken, and the emotional hurt can be devastating. The survivors may wish emotionally that one's loved one be not in that "better place" but rather with them right now. Because of the shock or denial of the death, the survivors may not have told certain heartfelt thoughts to the deceased while they were alive. There may have been places that they had wanted to visit with them, but now it is too late.

When we tell the grieving persons that the deceased is in a better place, it causes a "longing" even more for a connection with the loved one.

When my parents died, my friends would remind me that they were in a better place. I found myself wanting to exclaim, *"I don't care if they are better off, I want them with me, by my side, laughing, singing, and talking!"* I didn't want to be reminded that my loved one's body was in a casket and that he or she was in a better place.

Saying such can create hostility and resentment towards the deceased one:

"You are so selfish because now I have to do everything."
"How dare you die and leave me."
"Why didn't you confide in me about your illness?"
"I am so angry at you!"

Another way to express such a sentiment is as follows:

"I know you wish your loved one was face-to-face with you right now."

⟜

"It was God's will."

We use this expression as if God Himself whispered to a friend or a family member that it was His will to take the life of the beloved. Individuals will use God as part of their sentiments because it is as if using the name of God gives credibility and pure validation to the sentiment. Meaning well, people using this sentiment hope that it will comfort the survivor and that it will lessen the grief since God had a "hand" in the death.

If a loved one commits suicide, or dies due to some form of an accident, telling a bereaved person that it was God's will is ludicrous. Telling a bereaved person that God "willed" it to occur can cause the survivor to resent, and even blame God for the awful death.

While God is omniscient and knows when, where, and how we will make the transition, He does not cause the death but allows it.

⟜

"At least you can have other children."

Approaching the parents with this sentiment is uncalled for and may cause a potential outburst from the parents. They have just lost their most precious "gift" and do not need to be reminded that they can have more kids.

The sentiment sounds cold. Saying such demeans the death of the child. The dignity of and respect for the deceased child needs to be uplifted. A parent has had to say farewell to a child who no longer will be seated at the dinner table.

The very last thought in the minds of the parents is planning another child. The sorrowing parents are focusing on their loss. Their souls have hurtful bruises, and their souls need love, comfort, hope, and positive affirmations.

One of the most traumatic deaths is the sudden death of a child. The usual recovery requires a long period of time and effort. The parents may be grieving for many months or even years. They know that there can never be a substitution for their deceased loved one.

As supportive individuals, we need to give the parents lots of time before even suggesting that they begin doing things again, such as shopping or mixing socially.

"Time heals all pain."

It is true that time does heal or soften the pain. However, the survivor may not be ready to accept such a sentiment. His or her pain may be so intense that the individual does not believe that time is the answer.

When the survivor is in the beginning of the grief process, Time may be frozen. The survivor does not wish to think about the future of healing. They are barely able to focus on the present. The survivor may be asking oneself:

"How long will it take to be healed?"
"Why does it feel that time is my enemy?"
"Will I feel the pain lessening all at once or gradually?"

"How can I lessen the pain right now?"

Rather than telling the survivor that time heals
all pain, a suggestion is the following:

"Take your time healing. It will take place."

"I'm sure she is happy now."

When we say this sentiment to the survivors, they might think that
we are saying the deceased one was not happy until the death occurred.
This sentiment has an attached insinuation.

This sentiment may be accurate if the loved one has been in bad
health and in pain. One does not wish to witness the loved one in
misery, incapable of living life.

When the survivor is capable of "hearing" the message, the
sentiment of the loved one being happy can provide comfort. The
bereaved person can then believe the sentiment is true. This belief
can offer the bereaved moments of peace and of assurance. When this
is happening, the survivor can sense a healing. While the survivor is
feeling the healing, it is vital that loved ones stay in contact with the
person, long after the funeral.

Weeping is perhaps the most Human and
most universal of All relief measures.
—Karl Menninger

3

Death In A Family

The family does everything together from the beginning. Whatever the dad and mom decide on any given day, the children are certain to follow. This is the organized order in which we make sense of the family system. It isn't until many years later that the system begins to change. That happens when the children have been given permission by the parents to put their 2 cents worth into certain opinions and decision-making.

The family unit is the first educational institute that a child will be exposed to. The parents are the teachers who instruct their offspring about the elegance of life, profound respect for others, the daily responsibilities they are in charge of, their spiritual and familial heritage, etiquette, and so much more.

Children are taught the necessities of caring for those who comprise the family system. This obligation may occur at times slightly, such as when a family member contracts a bad cold or the nasty flu. When one of the parents undergoes a necessary operation, the siblings may need to pitch in and help.

One of the most crucial S.O.S. calls happens when one of the family members becomes terminally ill. This awakens all the senses of those who become caregivers. Whether it be the parent or child, the horrifying inner alarm sounds. The total dynamics and structure of the family system change drastically.

⌐∼

Grief is a process during which our minds grapple
with and find a way through the tumult of loss.
—Alexander Levy

⌐∼

It is important that every member of the family becomes a part of the care and well-being for the ill individual. When each individual has a significant role with the patient, a special bonding of caring and closeness is enacted and cemented. Each person can be responsible for doing certain tasks, such as providing water, dispensing the needed medication, or straightening up the bed. It is difficult enough that a family member is in dire straits, but to isolate one from the others can be catastrophic. Allowing all members to be a unit, a unified partnership, cements the relationships even tighter than it might have once been. Communication among all of the family can become an enriching learning procedure.

The terminally ill individual has much to tell the caregivers who make up his or her family, and may wish to share some of his or her sorrow with the siblings. Thoughts and emotions from the ill family member may be difficult to hear but are very important to be expressed.

It is not good to make a morgue out of one's home in the presence of the ill person. Normal activities, whenever possible, should continue to take place. By involving the ill individual, one does not send a "death" message that one's days on earth are ending. If the person is up to having visitors, then by all means, invitations should be issued. It can be quite rewarding to everyone being part of the visits.

⌐∼

Whatever method you choose, find a way to allow your
feelings to move from within yourself to outside yourself.
—James E. Miller

Continuing the family lifestyle, if possible, is a comfort to all the involved family members. If one is accustomed to watching certain television programs, continuing to do so is healthy. Most families have particular board games or other enjoyment activities that they are used to doing together, and these things have a calming impact on the family environment.

There will come a time in the life of the terminally ill when the final days are near. All of the family members should be allowed to participate as individuals and as the family unit. It is not unusual for the family to sing together their favorite songs while getting the ill person involved. Or, certain individuals may wish to say a prayer or to hold the ill patient or to be held. It is very important for the parents not to hide their grief with the hope of protecting their children.

Because of the tight bond, the individuals may wish to attend the funeral service and to visit the grave site. This should be allowed if requested. The individuals in the family may become very silent during this time, which is normal. The siblings well understand that the deceased person will not be attending their graduations, prom, or wedding. This hurts the bereaved—they are aching! Thus, silence takes over their personality.

Parents have the opportunity to teach their children about grief. One important way is that the parents need not hide their own personal grief reactions from their kids. It is okay—even healthy—for them to see their parents weep. Crying is not an embarrassment, but a healing.

Another way to teach children about the sadness of grief is to not camouflage the varied emotions surrounding grief. The children can learn that they are not obligated to plaster a smiling face on their countenance as if nothing tragic has occurred. Smiling faces are for happy moments in one's life, not for a significant death in the family arena. Parents and children are to be as "real" as possible, permitting current emotions to be the guide. Each person's reaction is about one's current grief!

When children are interviewed after the death of a parent, they often claim that they are the forgotten ones in the drama. The issue usually centers on the dying individual and on the surviving spouse. One possible explanation is the uneasiness of adult friends and relatives in talking about Death to a child and/or teenager. Also, the communication between the siblings may feel extremely awkward, new, and bothersome. In addition, adults can experience feelings of being completely out of one's comfort zone when talking about death. As an unfortunate result, conversations become disintegrated because "the players" are on totally opposite pages and on different communication patterns of thoughts and of emotions.

When dealing with children, there are several behavioral patterns that might be seen: one is the total silence at times down to the utterance of only a few words. This is normal behavior and needs to be respected. There will also be times when the bereaved may enter a withdrawal phase. It may seem as if the bereaved is being comatose or unfriendly. The reality is that the bereaved may be confused, frightened, or deep in grief. If the bereaved isolates oneself from others, there is no reason to panic. It's a defense mechanism and should not cause alarm as long as the isolation doesn't exists for months after the death. If it does, professional counseling might be needed.

It is not unusual if the bereaved child harbors feelings of guilt—believing that they are responsible for the death:

> ***"What did I do wrong?"***
> ***"What should I have done?"***
> ***"Was he mad at me?"***

At a young age, a child does not understand the dynamics of the dying process, and therefore the person will have dozens of questions. The inquiries need to be answered as best as possible, given the questions and the age of the child.

What can be harmful is pent up emotions infiltrating the mind of the child without a release. The bereaved needs "permission" to vent such feelings of sadness, anger, and guilt. If the death involved that of another sibling, the bereaved needs reassurances that the parents are still present to love and will continue to take care of their needs. If one of the parents died, then it's the responsibility of the surviving parent to reassure the children that the family will survive and regain itself.

There is absolutely nothing simple regarding the death of a loved one. It can become quite complicated and at times, mind-boggling. It is essential to take "one hour at a time" and do small "baby steps" while having to focus on what has taken place.

Bad things do happen; how I respond to them defines my character and the quality of my life.
—Walter Anderson

4

Traumatic Death

There is nothing easy or simple about facing a traumatic death. An actual death can be gut-wrenching, but adding trauma to the death creates a whiplash in one's soul. The soul becomes immediately shocked and void, without the essence of reality. The physical body becomes void of rational actions, while the mental state struggles desperately to make some type of sense of what has taken place.

"Trauma death" is a painful emotional experience or shock that may have a long lasting impact on the survivors. Family members may attempt to make rational sense of the trauma. The traumatic death leaves "soul bruises" in the daily lives of the survivors, and their attempt to process the event can be excruciating.

It's difficult at times to accept the "normal" procedure of a death. However, when the death is due to a traumatic event, such as a car accident or a drowning, or a bizarre, careless happening, every single element of our brain processing is tossed helter-skelter. We just can't make sense out of it. We don't seem capable of accepting the death. At the onset of the death, our shocked mind simply cannot wrap itself around the trauma.

Some individuals might refuse to accept the horrific traumatic death, thus not processing the feelings, thoughts, and gory images. They will bury deeply the trauma into their subconscious mind. Like a computer, the trauma may be "saved" until later in life until some act triggers the brain's memory center, and it spits out the memories surrounding the traumatic episode. When this happens, the outcome is a powerful set of raw emotions, such as anger, guilt, sadness, shame, and possibly fear. These unhealthy emotions have been festering inside the individual for months or possibly years. Their soul has become bruised from harboring such emotions.

Rather than dealing with the emotions surrounding the traumatic event, some individuals will hold prisoner the emotions for an indefinite period of time until possibly a specific song is heard that reminds them of the trauma, or they see a particular movie, or even have a conversation about the event...and the trigger is activated, releasing the emotional toxins. If the trauma is not mentally and emotionally conquered "face-to-face" it will exist inside the survivor, creating physical and emotional distress possibly for years.

Unexpressed emotions will never die. They are buried alive and will come forth later in uglier ways.
—Freud

If the survivor believes she or he caused the trauma, the emotion of guilt is horrendous. There doesn't seen to be any redemption. The survivor may believe she or he could have even prevented the traumatic death by being more alert, more conscientious, or more "on the ball" regarding the probability of the traumatic happening.

The devastation of guilt can tear through a person's soul. It leaves gigantic bruises on the soul and keeps the individual from enjoying life or finding peace within oneself. The guilt continues to gnaw at the person until the guilt is explored and handled correctly, usually with the assistance of a professional counselor.

The traumatized survivor may be trapped, almost frozen, within time and space. He or she can alternate between numbness and actually reliving the event. To reach healing, the survivor needs to access the trauma, which can be accomplished with a professional counselor. When the truth is finally recognized and dealt with, recovery can begin.

There are phone calls that I dread to receive. In the early hours or late at night, the shrill noise of the telephone awakened me from a deep slumber. I let it ring several times to tell if it was just a prank. As it continued to ring several more times, I feared the worst. I knew instinctively by what type of call comes in the middle of the night. It was always the very nature of the calls that seemed to stop my world and to put me on hold, like a busy clerk would do while I was trying to order some company merchandise.

The phone communication actually robbed me of a breath until I could wrap my mind around the earth-shattering message. The voice at the other end of the call was low, solemn, almost void of feeling. The deliverer of the information was experiencing extreme difficulty in vocalizing the traumatic news.

As I was processing the communication, my body had already begun responding. It was as if a cannonball had been aimed directly at my mid-section. With a verbal gasp, a cold shudder, and unforgettable shiver, my body seemed like it had completely separated from my mind, as if the physical had become an entity unto itself.

After a few moments of our connection, the caller hung up. With the phone still in my hand, I still could not register totally what I had just been told. His name was David. He was 16 years old and never got to see his 17th birthday. He loved life, and life loved him. He was intelligent, handsome, and well-liked by his peers and teachers. He had just one year left of his high school career. But on a late, rainy night, life for David came to a screeching halt. He would never see the next morning's sunrise. David died that night—alone. His new truck had skidded on a familiar curve into a tree that stood firm.

On that night, I got the call from a student which immobilized me for a few minutes. My mind could not wrap itself around what I just heard. As the school counselor, I knew David well. He had the tiger by the tail when I saw him just several days before he breathed his final breath.

The caller informed me that David's lifeless body had been routed to my nearby hospital, and his family and friends were gathering there now. I went to the hospital immediately.

What I saw in the waiting room was eerie. No one was talking. Everyone was staring at one another in shock and disbelief. Tears filled their weary eyes. The room's silence was deafening. Traumas, like this, just didn't happen in our small community. The atmosphere was surreal. Individuals were moving slowly around the room as if shackles were attached to their legs. All I knew at the time to do was blend in and become accessible.

The trauma was horrific for the community. David's untimely death colored the rest of the school year. Depression, guilt, anger, anxiety, and denial penetrated school and community events for the next year. David was not forgotten. He was praised by many, but sadly he never heard it.

When trauma of this magnitude takes place, the healing may have to come from outside sources because the entire community is hurt and devastated. The sources can be friends and relatives who live elsewhere and did not know David. A community trauma, like this, may require professionals who are trained to deal with such heart-breaking grief and hurt.

The regret of my life is that I have not
said, "I love you" often enough.
—Yoko Ono

5

Love Everlasting

These stories are straight from the hearts of the
adults who submitted them for publication in this
book. They are encouraging and challenging.

There is nothing more heart-breaking than that of a "soul death" – the
death of one who is intertwined in the lives of others. "Soul death" will
eventually happen, and we expect it. However, because we know it is
going to take place does not lessen the tremendous impact it has in our
lives. The following stories are of those who have experienced such a
"soul death", either physically or mentally.

My Name is Kennith

My name is Ken. I've been blind since birth, but it never stopped
me from having a wonderful, fulfilling seventy years on this beautiful
earth. My parents never allowed me to feel sorry for myself. Their
standards were just as high for me as they were for my younger sister,
Barbara. Within reason, what was expected of one held true for the
other. My folks demonstrated a phenomenal love for me, and along with
my precious sister, I had a team of cheerleaders who enabled me to be a
self-functioning individual in society.

Even though I was blind, God gave me a musical appreciation that
some folks with sight don't have. My keen sense of hearing allowed me

to hear the correct notes of songs and sing them perfectly on pitch. What an amazing gift was bestowed to me by my heavenly Father.

Because of my love for music and of my musical ability, I attended yearly music schools. I wish I could have seen the reactions of the other students who saw a blind man sitting right beside them, singing the music with perfect pitch while they were trying to learn the music through sight. I would have gotten a royal hoot out of that. I could always get my sister to take time out of her busy schedule to play the songs for me on our family piano. Music was an integral part of my life.

The quality, not the longevity, of one's life is what is important.
—Martin Luther King, Jr.

Speaking of my sister, Barbara and I had a truly amazing relationship. She never saw me as a blind person, but as simply her loving brother. We always had each other's back. We were genuine friends. Growing up through life to my last moments on earth, we were truly and always for each other. How many siblings can say that they call each other practically every single day? My sister and I did!

Often times she would read to me from her school textbooks which of course allowed me to learn a lot of information from those reading moments, and naturally it also helped her to learn the information.

My spiritual life kept me going when I wanted to give up. My Lord always reminded me through the lives of others that He was using me to carry out His marvelous plan...through me! I never believed I had the right to judge others or to be a critic. I accepted folks on their terms, and thus, I'm proud to say I had a lot of friends. I never once thought that God put me on earth to be someone's judge and jury. I was having too much fun being with people that being critical of them never really was of importance to me.

Both friends and strangers would often give me compliments because I was an "encourager" to them. I was indeed appreciative of such praise, but that it is God's will that we are all to be cheerleaders for one another. Some say that this is the Legacy that I left to them. I am proud of that!

What helped me spiritually was the small prayer altar that I built in the woods behind our home. It became my most favorite spot on the planet. Each day I'd go to my altar, get on my knees, and talk to God. Every single day at my altar was a highlight: it was just God and me.

When I had my stroke, my sister knew instinctively that I wasn't going to last much longer on earth. She just knew. Our kindred spirits were in touch with one another. After my passing, my sis lost some of her joy for life. Part of her left when I left. However, as the years have progressed, she re-located her inner joy through the love of her grandchildren and of course her great grandchildren. Sis would know that I wouldn't want her to put her life on hold because I can no longer answer her daily phone calls. Whatever she learned from my goodness and kindness and is now giving to others, that is what my Legacy to her is all about.

Once a year my church would have what is called a "Homecoming" in which people would come to pay their respects to those, like me, who have already passed on. For me, my passing is a "Home Going" because I am now "home" and while I miss being on earth, nothing can beat my new "home" with the Lord.

—*Barbara Long*

Lois—Mom and Hero
Lois was my mom, my friend, and my hero.
Mom was a vocal soloist, voice teacher, and church choir director. Other than her family, music was her whole world. When she was asked to sing a solo, the congregation would listen in awe at her beautiful voice. She was a true credit to the genre of Christian music.

Her faith was strong, and if anyone were around her for any length of time, the individual could sense her love for her Lord. Her tenacious faith was seen by my brother and me by the moral way she lived her life and also through the music that she dearly loved.

Mom, as well as Dad, taught us two "kids" that we could do anything in life we strived for. And each thing we worked at, Mom was our spiritual and parental cheerleader. She was so devoted to us. When my brother and I weren't successful at times, Mom would be ever-present to lift our spirits and to urge us to keep moving forward. She would not let us stay "down" because she knew of our capabilities.

Life for our family took a screeching halt in August of 2003. Mom had a debilitating stroke. She was unable to speak or sing. It was heartbreaking to see her trying to tell us something but unable to do so. My mom had a favorite Christian song ("The New 23rd") that she loved to sing as well as I do.

While she was in the hospital, I tried to sing to her...but I just couldn't. It was too painful for me, and I knew I'd break down and cry. Each time I thought I was ready, the words wouldn't come because of my intense grief and sadness. I just couldn't!

*It is during our darkest moments that
We must focus to see the light.*
---Aristole

As the weeks went on, Mom worked hard at her rehabilitation. Some speech returned, but I watched her utter frustration when the right words just wouldn't come to her. She tried so hard, but it was useless. I made sure she had her favorite CDs to listen to. Again, I tried to sing to her and still couldn't do it. There was too much emotion and love tied up to singing.

In October, more depressing news was told to us. Mom was having multiple seizures. However, her determination and commitment to "life" amazed all of us, including the doctors and nurses. Mom rallied and was able to leave the hospital to go to the nursing home. All of us felt an emotional relief.

But just a few weeks later, the debilitating seizures started again. We were devastated! Mom had lost her ability to swallow. The doctor wanted to put in a feeding tube. Mom heard the doctor's plan being explained to us, and she began to emphatically shake her head, "NO!" She wanted nothing whatsoever to do with a feeding tube even though it would have sustained her life for a few more months. As hard as it was, my father, my brother, and I supported her decision: **No Feeding Tube.**

My children wanted to visit Mom, so on a Sunday afternoon, we went. She was moving to Hospice the next day. She was visibly delighted to see us. Even though she still couldn't speak and had gotten extremely weak, her eyes lit up when we entered her hospital room. I had been praying over the issue of when to be very honest with mom and talk with her about her condition. So, with my kids there, I knew it was time. I took her frail hand.

"Mom, I know you are weary and worn out. One day soon you will be singing with the angels."

She gripped my hand, smiled at me, and nodded her head. Beyond a shadow of a doubt, I believe she knew exactly what was going on, and she knew where she was going! Heaven-bound.

At that moment, I knew that I could sing to her. I was able to sing her favorite song, "The New 23rd" without any hesitation. I sang to my mom, and knew that it would probably be the last time. It just had to be God giving me strength and singing through me.

When I had finished, my children shared with Mom their special memories of her involvement with them of years gone by. We took each other's hand and prayed together. It was an astounding experience!

Because of our devoted love for Mom, my brother and I seldom left her side. I was sleeping in the Hospice room. My brother and I were totally exhausted. We were convinced by a family member to go to my brother's home for a night of rest and sleep.

During the night, Mom passed into her new "home" with her Lord. I was devastated that I had left her side on the night she died. A close friend helped me to understand the dynamics of Mom's death: *"Joy, your mom wanted to spare you the trauma of her dying while you were with her. She knew how difficult it would have been on your brother and you. Joy, she waited until your brother and you were gone. She simply did not want to die in your presence."*

Once again, Mom was thinking about my brother and me rather than herself. Her last moments on earth were about us! And now she is singing once again--in the heavenly choir, where we will join her one day.

—*Joy Breedlove*

⌁

We do not remember days, we remember moments.
—Cesare Pavese

⌁

My Loving Mom
Within months of each other, I lost my dad from brain cancer and my mom from lung cancer. I didn't have a chance to finalize my grieving about Dad before I was hit with another whammy with my mom's passing. Both parents left much too early, leaving me as an adult orphan. No one can have two such tragedies that close together without feeling angry, morose, and depressed. So, I ended up having to plow through two simultaneous episodes of the grieving stages. I wasn't able to see a bright spot anywhere in my life with the deaths of my wonderful parents.

Of the two deaths, losing my Mom was the hardest. I think it was the worse because Mom's personality and mine were so different, unlike my Dad and me.

Mom could brighten up almost everyone's day with her caring and loving personality. She and I had so many good times together, doing mundane chores as well as the more serious responsibilities. I loved

Mom deeply and miss her presence in my life and in the life of her grandchildren.

One of the times that I miss her most is at Christmas. Mom loved to cook and to decorate the house with Christmas ornaments. Plus, she wanted all of us to be with her during the holiday season. My siblings and I would pull fun pranks on each other or on Mom. We were very, very cautious when opening our individual gifts because we weren't sure if we were to become a Christmas victim. My mom loved to watch the "show" among her kids. Of course she was eligible to become a victim too. With my family at Christmas especially, no one but no one could see the pranks coming. Nobody was excused from a probable prank in our household.

Even though I now have my own family with whom to celebrate, Christmas is different now. Mentally I can still see Mom in the room while my own family are opening their gifts. I keep waiting for my wife or my two beautiful girls to even pull a prank. No telling where they learned to do such?

When Mom found out about her illness, she pretended that she was fine and well. She put on a good show of deceit. She knew that if we found out, everyone in the family would be worried and depressed.

The Key To Immortality Is First Living A Life Worth Remembering.
—Bruce Lee

All of us knew that something was wrong. It was too obvious. And then one day, my world became shattered. We were told the whole truth. The news was devastating! I suspected that Mom knew her illness was terminal. All of us were trying to get through Dad's death and now, we had to face the horrible death of my Mom. It was most difficult working though Dad's grief stages and now we had another one with which to deal.

Mom believed in family traditions and expected us to enact them. The traditions went from minor to major ones. A minor one may be to attend church each week. A major one might be to schedule being with all the family on Christmas morning.

My profound regret is that my Mom didn't have the opportunity to see my two daughters. They were yet to be born at the time of Mom's death. Knowing my Mom, she would have absolutely spoiled them rotten to the core.

I know that my Mom would have been an awesome grandmom. Her sense of humor and her smile would have captivated my girls. If my daughters had pulled a dozen pranks on my Mom, she would have enjoyed every single prank.

I miss Mom's love and attention that she gave me with absolutely no strings attached.

Even though I get lots of love and attention from my family, the love that comes from one's mom is somehow different.

Mom was my biggest cheerleader. I miss her encouragement and her available presence. She taught me so much about "life" and I wish I could thank her again. I am very fortunate to have had her caliber of character in my life.

Thanks, Mom.

—*Kelly Taylor*

MOM—A "Lost" Soul

The adult child becomes eventually the parent when one of the several brain disorders traps the true parent into confusion and dismay. This is what happened in my own family. My mom lived life to its fullest, and those who were a part in her arena loved Mom's keen sense of humor and carefree personality. She was a genuine hoot! One could not be around my mom for long before each individual was laughing and cutting up with her. She could be quick-on-the-draw in responding to people's questions about life. Maybe people surrounded her due to the pure love shining through her caring personality. She was an amazing person, and yes, I may be biased, but that does not change the truth that she was phenomenal in every aspect of her personality. She was considered an icon in her school environment with administrators, teachers, and the students. She worked magic with the students. They respected and loved her because she was their personal cheerleader, plus caring for each single one. As her daughter, people constantly tell me stories about what she did for them that I never knew.

The next group of folks she loved was her family. Mom was always available to me when I was growing up. Like all mothers and daughters, we had our problems, but I could always depend on her word to be carried through. If she promised me something, I knew that she would make it happen or at least attempt to.

Her mental disorder, Dementia, is wicked. There are times when I go to visit her in the nursing home that I can't wake her up because it's as if she is in a deep coma. When I experience such a situation, I feel as if I've lost her for sure. But she eventually comes out of her deep slumber and gives me a beautiful smile. Some days she doesn't talk much, but she knows the people who are there in the room with her. She can't communicate her thoughts very well, but her eyes speak volumes.

Almost every day a family member visits her. She still recognizes each of us. She loves it when she is taken outside to see, feel, and hear the various sounds of nature. She almost becomes a totally different person when we are outdoors. Her spirit soars like a beautiful eagle. Watching birds is one of her favorite things to do. I can see the change in her eyes. We sit and talk about mundane things. I'm very careful about what I say to her, so as not to upset her. Each time, before I leave her, I give her a big hug because I love her so much. She hugs me back, and then we go back inside.

While Mom's mind no longer belongs to her, she can still tickle me with her wit. Soon after she has forgotten what she has said, I can still be laughing long after the occurrence.

Individuals, like Mom, have what is called "sun downers" --during the day hours, she seems to be okay within reason. When the sun begins to go down, Mom can become scared, confused, agitated, and unsettled. It is difficult for me emotionally watching her in such a state of mind. I attempt to comfort her. Sometimes I'm successful while other times I can't get past "the barrier" in which she is living.

Mom has always been my life's icon. She was my cheerleader, my motivator, and my hero. Now, it's time that I am her encourager and her strength. I deem it a privilege to have such a role. Mom gave her all to me, and now it's my turn to do it for her.

Thanks, Mom, for everything.

—*Lyn George Harbin*

P. S.
Mom passed away on May 28, 2018, just before publication of this book.

MY ANGEL

My daughter, Audrianna, passed away at age thirteen, two weeks before her fourteenth birthday. My world was shattered into little pieces, and my heart broke.

Audrianna was the type of person who could walk into a room of people, and take over. She brought an energetic source into the room, and everyone was awed by her personality. She had the ability to put people at ease by entertaining them to a point of having everybody laughing at something she said or did. Audrianna was a genuine entertainer.

When she was seven, an artificial heart valve had to be implanted in her tiny chest. Of course this caused her to be very careful of not overexerting herself. There were things that her friends could do that she couldn't, but she accepted that reality. She would cheer them on, and that role suited her fine. She knew eventually that she would outgrow her heart valve, and it would have to be replaced with a larger one.

The day of the surgery arrived, and we were all in good spirits. The nurses prepped Audrianna, and I gave her a big hug and kiss before she was wheeled into the surgical room.

Since my family had already gone through Audrianna's first surgery, we kind of knew the pre-op and post-op scheduling. We knew approximately when we would be seeing her in the recovery room.

We were informed of when the operation was finished. We knew that we would be joining her in the recovery room soon. One hour went by—no word. Two hours—no word. When the third hour came and vanished, I knew that something was drastically wrong. I felt it.

Finally when I was allowed to see Audrianna, the scene looked like it came straight from a scary Hollywood movie. She was hooked up to machine after machine upon machine. My sweet baby was still unconscious and thus had no inkling of how she looked or what she was hooked up to. I couldn't believe what I was actually witnessing. Because of her high fever, she was "packed" in ice.

I've cried, and you'd think I'd be better for it, but the sadness just sleeps, and it stays in my spine the rest of my life.
—Conor Oberst

I found out that during the operation, Audrianna was given the wrong blood thinning medication which caused all of her organs to shut down. During all of the trauma, she did open her beautiful eyes for about 30 seconds, and then closed them for eternity.

Even though it has been several years since her death, to me, it still feels like it was yesterday. There are times when I just need to feel close to my angel, so I get some of her clothes out and smell them. I can still actually smell her scent, even to this day, and that is what I am grateful for. Audrianna will always be with me. Our spirits will always soar together, and there will never be a time that I am not her mom.

I miss you, Audrianna, and always will.

Your Mom
Angel Sprayberry

Jennifer--My Active Daughter

My name is Jennifer, and I was almost fourteen years old when my fun-filled life ended. I lived my life to the fullest, and I mean the fullest. One of my favorite hobbies was drawing whatever pictures would come to my mind, which were many. I kept some for my own private collection while others were given to those who expressed an interest.

My main cheerleader in life was my fabulous mom. I loved her so much. She and I could connect without using words—our eyes and facial expressions communicated volumes of information to each other. I'm sure my step-dad wondered what we were communicating, but his great sense of humor just accepted it for what it was—a phenomenal relationship between a mother and her daughter.

I put a painting of mine under my bed that was for mom to find. It was an art work that expressed my deep love for her. Little did we know that it was to be my last drawing: it was done the day before I left earth to be with God. At the time I drew it, I guessed I had planned to eventually give it to her, so I put it under my bed for safe-keeping. Mom discovered it the day after my funeral.

I think it's interesting that we believe that we have all the time in the world to tell people of our love for them without fully understanding that we are not really guaranteed a tomorrow.

"Mom, I know you will treasure my drawing of love dedicated to you."

I loved animals. Even though my asthma posed a problem of allergic reactions, that didn't stop me from being around them and of course hugging every single one. If I came across an ill animal, asthma or not, my mission was to save the precious creature.

What I wanted to have was a farm when I grew up. My goal was to have lots and lots of cows, horses, goats, and chickens. Of course other animals were welcomed, such as dogs, cats, and rabbits. Speaking of rabbits, I had a precious one for 13 years! Yes, 13 wonderful years. We were pals together. My rabbit died a few months after I did. I think that our pets can grieve over our deaths. They can sense something is wrong when their "master" is no longer in sight. Thus, they grieve themselves-to-death. At least this is what I believe personally.

I knew that I had physical limitations in life as to what I could do without stirring up an asthma attack. But I chose not to complain about it because who wants to be around a whiner? Besides, I had my video games and pets for indoor fun and my 4-Wheeler and my garden for outdoor activities. I really had it made.

―――

Grief is the last act of love we have to give to those we loved. Where there is deep grief, there was great love.
—Anonymous

―――

My journey to heaven started around one o'clock in the morning. I woke from my sleep, unable to breathe. I was having a full blown asthmatic attack. Mom knew immediately that I needed to go to the hospital.

My step-dad was driving as fast as he could while Mom was in the back seat with me. She was holding me in her arms and talking softly to me. On the way to the hospital with Mom holding me, I passed gently into glory.

Mom knew instinctively that I had just left my "outward covering" here while my spirit was with God.

Even though it has been several years since my departure, Mom is still dealing with my death. We were such great companions in life with many, many wonderful adventures together. She is still somewhat grieving the loss.

Mom likes telling people that I was the one who taught her what real "life" was all about. Not sure what things I taught her, but I am glad to have left such a vibrant legacy. This is the greatest validation of living I could have ever wanted.

—*Annette Russell Franklin*

―――

Steve, My Love

Life changes in a blink of an eye. I never thought I would face my husband's death at this stage of life. Instead of considering the possibility of death, we were planning for retirement and enjoying life with each other, not considering a funeral. We were thrust into a situation where we could not change the outcome. The doctor's words hit me like a ton of bricks, taking my breath away. My husband, Steve, sat emotionless staring at the wall.

Steve had undergone an MRI that morning. Although Steve never voiced his worries, he knew deep down in his soul something was seriously wrong. The MRI showed that he had glioblastoma (brain tumor).The doctor told Steve that he could be kept comfortable, but there was no cure.

Our lives became a whirlwind of confusion, of unbelief. On our way home from the doctor's office, I thought: *"This was not happening!" "Did I hear correctly?" "How do others handle devastating news that changes the course of life?"* and *"Why? Why? Why?"* It was a very silent ride home.

Once we got home, I unplugged all the phones and sat on the couch. I broke down and cried buckets of tears. As Steve looked at me, I told him that I did not want to lose him. He was my love.

The following day we sat in the oncologist's office, waiting for the verdict. I told Steve that whatever came our way, we would fight it together. This diagnosis came just as we were beginning to talk about our future together. Steve had talked about retirement, and we had planned to travel, to see the world, and to rediscover each other. To me, this situation that we were in was unfair, and I felt we had been cheated of a happy life together. I knew the road ahead of us would be rough, but I never gave up hope.

After our oncologist reviewed the MRI and confirmed the diagnosis, he talked about options. Prognosis was grim. Not only was it brain cancer, but it was very large. It took up the whole left hemisphere of the brain: thereby, it affected his speech, emotions, decision-making, balance, as well as the right side of his body.

My question was *"How long had Steve had this cancer?" " Did I miss something?" "If we had caught it earlier, would it have made a difference?"*

The doctor communicated that Steve probably had the cancer for only six weeks. Glioblastoma is a very aggressive, fast-growing cancer. When the doctor talked about life expectancy, he talked in months, not in years.

The first step for lengthening life expectancy was surgery to remove as much of the tumor as possible. Without surgery, life expectancy was 2 months. With surgery, 12 to 15 months were possible. I looked at Steve and begged him to fight for me. He nodded his head, and I told the doctor to make arrangements for surgery.

For the second time, I felt the sting of the words "terminal" and "death".

When our son, Kalem, walked through the door after hearing about his father's situation, Steve was sitting in his usual spot on the couch. The term glioblastoma brain cancer registered a shock across our son's face. He could not comprehend the magnitude of the conversation—no cure, surgery in 2 days, life expectancy. Words rushed at him like a broken dam.

I walked my son out to the car, and he fell against my chest and cried. I wrapped my arms around him, kissed him on the head, and whispered, *"We will get through this."* It was hard for our son to leave. He felt he needed to be with his dad during this life-shattering time.

We all could see a decline in Steve's mobility and speech on an almost daily basis. One night Steve fell against the wall as he tried to get into bed. This scared me to my very toes.

Two days later we were sitting in the surgery unit waiting for Steve's surgery time. Surgery seemed to take forever. The surgeon confirmed the mass as a very large glioblastoma. The tumor took up most of Steve's left hemisphere and only ten percent could be removed. We tried to console one another.

Our son was mad at the world, at God, and at life. He had just started his new career, and he wanted his dad to be part of his new adventure. Kalem wanted to share his experiences with his dad, and he still needed his dad's guidance and advice on life.

Those nights in ICU were emotionally and physically draining. I didn't get much rest between sleeping in the recliner and the nurses coming in every hour to take care of Steve.

Over the next several weeks, Steve became less and less mobile at home and virtually non-verbal. Several times I had to call 911 to help get Steve off the floor from where he fell as he tried to get up. My parents moved in with us to help lessen the physical load and mental stress.

Death Ends A Life, Not A Relationship.
—Mitch Albom

I would continue to struggle daily with Steve's day-to-day care. The last week of Steve's life started out as pure chaos. My husband was getting weaker. One night as I was taking my shower, I fell to my knees, my eyes filled with tears, and I prayed for a miracle. Except this time, my prayer was not on healing but on peace. I asked the Lord to please not let Steve suffer. If Steve could not be healed, please take him quickly. Please don't allow him to suffer as so many people do with this horrible disease.

Two months to the day of Steve's surgery, we were in the emergency room. The ER doctor met me in the hall to discuss the results of the CT scan. The waves kept hitting me with what the doctor was verbalizing. I couldn't even catch my breath before the next wave hit me. I was drowning. I couldn't comprehend the ER doctor's words, "*Steve is dying. He could die within the next hour. If you have family members you need to call, you need to call them now.*"

Steve was moved to a private hospital room and hospice was called. Steve's breathing was shallow, and he had the death rattle sound. Steve was too weak to speak, but he knew what was happening. Family and friends came to the hospital to say their good-byes, and all Steve could do was to try to nod. Instead of holding Steve's hand throughout that evening, I was making decisions with hospice and making arrangements for the impending event.

I learned from the hospice nurse that the hearing is the last thing to go before someone passes. Once everyone left, I whispered into Steve's ear that he was my true love and that I would be all right. Steve's steady death rattle was like the sound of an ocean wave washing against the beach. Around 3:00 A.M., Steve took his last breath. The hospital room was filled with eerie silence. Steve was finally at peace. He didn't want to leave his life, but neither would he have wanted to stay in his sick body.

The next several days I was consumed with funeral arrangements. I had great family and friend support. People wanted to help, but they didn't know what to do. There are no words of comfort and no one knows what to say. The most comfort was just having people come to visit.

After the funeral, the week-ends were lonely. This was a road I had to travel alone. As long as someone was with me, I wouldn't deal with my raw emotions. I packed my feelings in a suitcase and stored them under the bed until I could privately suffer with them. No one can make losing a spouse any easier for you.

I had to work through my feelings of "This is not fair, why me?" I had regrets and guilt to work through. I had guilt over why did I not notice subtle changes in Steve earlier. I had guilt over not being the perfect wife. I had guilt over not encouraging Steve to retire so we could enjoy the life we had. I had guilt over getting irritated at him for things he didn't have control over during his illness. I had plenty of guilt to go around and the "what ifs" were eating me up. I finally realized the decisions that I made were based on the information I had at the time. I made the best decisions I could at those moments.

There were many nights I cried until I couldn't breathe. I cried to God for answers. The key to my surviving the loss of my spouse was to get involved with life again. I had to stay busy and work on myself to become a better me. No, life is not the same, but it is what we make of it. I could not go on day-to-day in such a miserable state. I will always love Steve. We produced a great son together. Steve will always be a part of me, but I knew he would not want me to give up on life.

From Steve's death, I learned many lessons about love. Some lessons were learned too late. I learned to make sure others in one's life hear "**I love you**" often. I learned to be more kind and more patient. I learned to make the other person feel as if they were the most important person in the world and to put their feelings first. Criticize little and love more. I learned that most things in life are not worth arguing over. I learned to never leave things unsaid and to discuss the hard issues. I learned life is short and tomorrow is never promised. Therefore, make the most of your time together with family and friends.

—Angie Burns

I can choose to rise from the pain and treasure the most precious gift I have—life itself.
—Walter Anderson

6

Death of a Parent

Our parents have always been by our side since the beginning of our existence on earth, and it is the reason of one's deep hurt and sorrow when they each pass away. They are irreplaceable—no longer available for us to call or to visit. Our "inner" child grieves deeply because the child has now become an orphan. Our "adult" self can also feel intense, emotional hurt and pain.

When we are alone and meditating on their deaths, memories flood us. We learned about life from them. Our first learning"institution" is the parents. We learned what social skills were needed to "make it" in our society. Since the home is where our educational system started, we have many positive memories that can give us comfort and healing.

The relationship is unique in that it was where we first experienced unconditional love. As children, we believed that our parents would love and accept us no matter what we did—pure love without attached conditions. Losing the two people who gave us so much can be horribly traumatic.

Dealing with our own mortality might occur when we are experiencing their specific deaths. We may try to figure out our own longevity by the ages our parents were when they died.

The ache over their deaths is normal and necessary in order to muddle through the grieving process. When my parents passed on, I could remind myself of their loyalty, their love, and their support. It was my honor to have them as parents, and that honor does not go away at the time of their deaths. It lives forever within me.

Because our parents are central figures in life, the sudden or unanticipated death of a parent is a shock. We lose his or her physical presence, and a part of one's self is gone. We can feel it deep within our spirit that something is just not the same anymore.

When the second parent dies, we go through the exhaustive emotions once again. We realize that we no longer have the "home" to visit again. Our parents were the ones to make the "home" what it was, and thus, "home" went with them. We may feel "orphaned" and some of the feelings can be anger at the parents for leaving us.

Our grief over the deaths of our parents is unique indeed from those deaths of others in our lives. All about us are memories of our parents—pictures, particular songs, bequeathed furniture, favorite television shows—all of these will activate certain memories we had with our parents. Thus, the personal loss is profound. Their deaths can strike intense grief. We can feel the grief of unfinished business we had with them. Perhaps we didn't visit them near enough or we had a terrible argument with them and didn't get it resolved before their deaths. All of these can create horrible grief and guilt. These emotions may be coming from our "inner" child rather than the adult. The "child" becomes frightened because being an orphan is devastating.

If the parent is suffering from a terminal illness, the adult may have to be the caregiver. It becomes emotionally difficult watching our ill parent slowly decline. We witness their lack of energy, the horrific pain, the mental lapses, and possibly the non-existent communication. A role reversal takes place. The parent becomes the "child" and we become the "parent" in the arena. We may have to handle things that once belonged to our parents, such as finances, legal matters, and medical responsibilities.

As a result of becoming the caregiver, our lives may be put "on hold" until the parent passes. As the caregiver, we may experience anxiety, even questioning our ability to be responsible for the caring of the parent. Another feeling may be resentment and anger at having to give up one's "life" to take care of the parent.

When family members are being the caregivers, there is a perpetual sadness about losing a loved one. Such sadness may be hidden, but each person aches all over. They know of the impending doom. There are feelings that may accompany the sadness, such as dread, guilt, and helplessness. Furthermore, the bottom line of such sadness is that it mutilates one's energy level. Also, it has a powerful impact on us physically, mentally, emotionally, socially, and spiritually.

We caregivers will experience being drained physically. Because of this, caregivers need to "escape" at times when at all possible. The "escape" can be going to a movie, to a concert, a luncheon, or a walk of solitude. This is not dishonoring the one who is ill. It is a breath of deliverance to enrich oneself, to maintain one's health and well-being, and to be refreshed in order to return to the "battleground" with one's coping skills.

When the parent passes, it impacts the entire family system if children are still in the home. It upsets the balance because a key player is no longer present to assume his or her role. Due to the balance shifting as individuals must assume different roles, there will be problems of adjustment. This is natural and normal.

It is of great importance, after the death, that each family member be totally free to acknowledge the loss in his or her way. The individual may feel that there was unfinished business to conduct before the death but didn't do it. Thoughts, feelings, and actions were not completed or the "if onlys" and "should haves" create tremendous guilt. The family member needs to voice this without fear of condemnation or judgment.

Expressing one's grief emotions is a vital part of the bereavement process. It has to be done, or else the individual will have an extremely difficult time transitioning from one step of the grieving process to the next step. Promoting the real emotions, whether negative or positive, needs to be encouraged throughout the family system. It's healthy to be genuine!

Each family member may wish to commemorate the loss in different ways. Therefore, it is important that family members have the opportunity of planning the viewing, the funeral, and the grave site service. When only one person does it all, hurt feelings and attitudes can happen.

The grief over the death of a parent can be gut-wrenching. The pain hurts deeply, at times seemingly taking our breath away. Overwhelming grief is an ongoing process until the person has finally finished the bereavement journey. In the meantime, grief cuts through our capacity for pleasure. Sometimes the survivors will have difficulty in concentrating on anything but mundane tasks. The grief sets up a barricade, preventing us at times doing our main responsibilities in the family. However, there is always the quality of hope and assurance that will help to carry us along on our bereavement journey.

I would rather die a meaningful death
than to live a meaningless life.
—Corazon Aquino

Parents are a stabilizing presence; they are keepers of our
history and childhood; they are our connection to the past;
they are our cheerleaders; they are our most profound source
of acceptance and unconditional love. When a parent
dies, then, all of these things are torn at the seams.
—Alan D. Wolfelt

7

Death of a Spouse

"Until death do we part"...when newlyweds make this promise to one another on their wedding day, it is more than likely just words of intent. At the time, a death is a far away idea from their minds. They envision years upon years of being as "one" with a bonding love and genuine acceptance of one another. Their thoughts of being together forever are cemented into their newlywed minds as they begin their journey together.

For however long their marriage lasts, an impending death or a sudden demise can be horrific. The marital relationship is cracked wide open, and like Humpty Dumpty, it can't be put together as it once was.

When one of the spouses dies, the surviving one may feel adrift and incapacitated. Being emotionally alone becomes one's reality. If one of the spouses has a terminal illness and is hurting relentlessly, the other mate may be relieved after the loved one's demise. No longer does the mate have to watch his or her spouse suffer in agony and pain.

If the husband passes away first, the wife will come face-to-face with a boat-load of changes in the household arena. Whatever responsibilities the husband had in the household will fall completely on the wife. There may be some responsibilities that she had no idea of the way to handle, such as organizing family finances, doing lawn care, or repairing certain items.

On a gut level, the wife may start having panic attacks stemming from the significant loss of security that her husband had given her.

Whatever level of dependence she had with her loved one has ended with his death. She has to fend for herself as the sole adult in her home. Even if there are children still in the home, the surviving spouse is still in charge of what is going on in the house.

The mother will have to undertake the more serious responsibilities. In order to do the necessary chores, she will have to adjust her personal schedule to get "everything known to mankind" done—daily.

The wife becomes the "lone" parent. Life activities surround her. This can be quite overwhelming, leading to acute loneliness and depression.

The spouse soon learns that she can't do everything to keep the family functioning. She may need to stop doing certain tasks in order to get other things accomplished. In addition, she may need to delegate specific responsibilities to the children, if any are still in the home.

Assistance from friends and relatives can be a welcomed answer to prayer. Meals need to be prepared even long after the loss. It becomes a gracious act from those who are in the trenches with the spouse.

Babysitting the children so the spouse can have some relief time is another way of easing the spouse's burden of grief. Whatever the spouse selects to do during the relief time is a personal decision which needs to be encouraged by family members and friends. No spouse can operate effectively 24/7, week upon week without some allocated time for self. It is a necessity for good mental health.

Life is short, and we should respect every moment of it.
—Orhan Pamuk

When the wife dies first, there can be also a dramatic change in the family system if children are still at home. The husband's schedule may be less flexible than that of the wife. If it is, then the father is faced with several dilemmas:

"How do I re-invent my schedule?"
"How can I run the errands that my wife once did?"
"When can I do my chores and hers?"
"Who is available to help with the children?"
"How do I handle this role reversal?"

Due to all the dilemmas that need answering, it is not uncommon for the father to have possible resentment towards his wife for dying and leaving him all the dilemmas. Some emotions and thoughts don't make sense at times, such as the resentment. However, one must own such feelings in order to deal with them adequately.

The father has to deal with the ever-present world of his children— mainly alone. Dealing with school issues, shopping, and all sorts of appointments now belongs to the father. If the father doesn't ventilate his feelings via a friend or a professional, then he is doomed to possible clinical depression. The needs of the family will change drastically once a spouse passes away.

"Who is going to take up the slack?"
"What is now my role in the family?"
"How do I get where I'm supposed to be all the time?"

There will be ups and downs as each family member finds his or her new place in the family system. This change of roles may take months before each person is comfortable. This cannot be rushed!

If there are no children remaining in the home, the spouse can still be devastated over the role reversal. The spouse realizes that being alone is now the new lifestyle. The loved one is no longer available to be by the spouse's side—to encourage, to love, to share thoughts, to just be present.

The death will have an impact on the spouse's social situation. Because a significant individual is no longer available, the remaining spouse must re-learn how to relate to one's new social world. New interests may be on the horizon. There is the probability that the old friends will be put on the shelf and new ones formed.

Re-learning one's social world can be awkward and scary at times, but it can also be exciting and encouraging.

The spouse may have the tendency to become a recluse. This is the time when friends and family members can rescue the spouse by introducing her or him to the new social arena. At first baby steps need to be taken. As time passes, the spouse will let the supportive individual know when he or she is ready to move a little faster into the social dimension.

8

Death of a Child

The call to my home came late at night. The voice on the other end was hysterical, and far beyond frantic sobs. I could only understand a few scattered words: accident, dead, ambulance, emergency room.

And then I heard the name of one of my students, and my world stopped. My mind could not process what I was was being told: a death had occurred. It was only moments after the call that I realized what I had heard, and out the door I headed to the hospital.

When I entered the emergency room, the environment seemed surreal: students quietly crying, adults whispering to one another, nurses in and out monitoring the situation of the bereaved, and the mother of the student looking shocked.

When the nurse appeared finally to the mother to tell her that her deceased son could be viewed, the mother grabbed my hand to go with her. The boy was in a black body bag. As we watch the attendant unzip the bag, the mother's hand tightened on mine.

The boy was a handsome, lovable young man. He and I had grown close to each other as high school counselor and student. We had genuine respect for each other. And now I was looking down at a promising young student who would never again see daylight or see his life goals reached. I was heart-broken.

A death in a school community shakes the very foundation of such an institution. In a small populated school, the death has an impact to some degree on every single student, teacher, and school personnel. There is no possible way to be immune from such devastation. It just cannot happen.

When such a death is unexpected, the range of emotions among everyone can go from shock and denial to pure, unadulterated hysteria in a heartbeat. Sudden deaths boggle the mind while the emotions become uncontrollable. Whether by an accident or suicide, we are not prepared, especially when the death is a student: a child, a pre-teen, or a teenager. We just aren't ready for such a shock.

When a dysfunctional person(s) murders the lives of those in the school community, the utter devastation of the survivors can exist for years, especially if they witnessed the onslaught. Therefore, whether the death is sudden or violent, there is no-easy-way-out in the lives who make up the school arena. Everyone suffers!

Because of the trauma, many times the school personnel and the students must have professional assistance. Social workers, school counselors, and other professional personnel are available to help diminish the shock, to soothe the hurt, and to guide the survivors to some degree of acceptance.

Martha Oates, in her book, <u>Death in the School Community</u>, quoted a letter from Chee-yun, a 16 year-old, who wrote this letter to her boyfriend who was killed in an automobile accident:

"I still miss you even though it has been a year. Sometimes I relive the accident.

It goes over and over again in my head. When you died, I felt as if something that belonged to me and only me had been taken away. I was mad at first. I was mad at you for leaving and at God for taking you. My life is not the same. I wish I had said that I loved you more often and had let you know how much I cared for you. I miss and love you very much."

Attempting to sweep the death of a student under the rug is a gigantic mistake. On February 14, 2018, one of the world's deadliest school massacres happened in Parkland, Florida. Students need to express their grief about the deaths. If they need to cry, to scream, or even to laugh about their memories of their deceased friends, then it needs to take place.

Steps of Helping Those Who Are Grieving

Immediately after the death, the affected students and school personnel need to process their feelings and thoughts with a professional facilitator.

- The facilitator needs to encourage each individual to express themselves as best they can.
- The facilitator needs to explain the grief stages that the grievers will have to journey through.
- The facilitator needs to provide coping strategies to the students and school personnel.
- There must be a follow-up plan for the grievers.

Death does not take a holiday from students simply because the individual is labeled a school student. In many school communities, each year the school will experience at least one death by means of an automobile accident, a suicide, or a terminal illness. It will be heartbreaking, earth-shattering, and down right gut wrenching.

Parents can be of assistance in the school community when a death has occurred. Each school usually welcomes calls from parents who wish to assist the students and school personnel. You, as a parent, can be an angel in disguise in the school community. Making oneself available is a genuine sign of kindness, compassion, and love for the school community.

Fred had a loving five-year-old son. On a hectic morning, Fred had no inkling that his son was moving his toy bike out from behind Daddy's big truck. Fred was in a hurry. His son wasn't.

Such a tragedy has all the potential of catapulting the lives of family members into a nightmarish world that is filled with every negative emotion known to mankind. Fred and his family members will never be the same; their world has changed permanently. Life as they once knew it cannot be restored to what it once was because their world is now missing a vital person—a son who brought laughter, joy, and happiness into the family circle. For certain, it was an accident. But with an untimely death, the guilt begins.

The death of a parent's child, no matter what the age, is devastating. According to the "parental philosophy" the parents were expected to die first, most certainly not the child. It is a heart-breaking situation when the parents are having to attend the funeral of their child. The struggle to understand the dynamics becomes almost impossible. And the recovery period seems like eternity. One of the heart-beats of the family has been forever quieted.

If the child is dying from a terminal illness, he or she may have an inner awareness of the impending death. The child can sense it coming. Some children may even want to discuss "death and its dynamics" with the parents who are in denial.

If the parents are not ready to be engaged in such a discussion, the child may reach out to others who will listen, such as a special friend or even the roommate in the hospital. The individual has much to talk about and needs to be free to express oneself. The conversation can help to reduce anxieties the child has about the dying process and of death.

Most children believe in a better place that they are traveling to. The belief in a Heaven becomes important to the child. The child may wonder if he or she will still be experiencing pain while in Heaven or what will Heaven look like. The child may need the parents' answers to these questions.

It is not unusual for a parent to find a poem, or a drawing, or a letter that the child composed about death. In the written communication may be the child's insights and other interesting comments that the child has expressed concerning his or her demise.

The death will cause the family structure to come to a crashing halt for the time-being. The healthy siblings will need the opportunity to vent their feelings. If not with the parent, this can be done with a good friend, a caring adult who knows the family, or even a professional caregiver. The siblings, like their dying sibling, also need attention. They are going through a nightmare in which they experience confusion, guilt, worry, and even anger. Venting is healthy. The siblings should be allowed to feel every emotion without condemnation or judgment. Crying out their pain and shedding a boat-load of tears are a realistic and healthy means to recovery.

If the child's death is sudden, without any warning, the shock can be mind-boggling. Confusion can take over rational thinking. The grief becomes unbearable. There was no time to say good-bye or to give a last hug. The death could have been gruesome, such as a drowning or a car accident. This type of death causes the loved ones deep anguish, and one's imagination pictures the horrible death. Some family members never recover fully from this form of grief and hurt. Their grief becomes unmanageable. This type of sudden death impacts the family in different ways than an anticipated death. The journey to acceptance resembles a roller coaster ride. The twists and turns are many and unexpected.

The parents may wonder what the child would have become if the death had not occurred. Many thoughts about the child will flood the minds of each parent which can intensify the grief and hurt. The parents may blame themselves or each other for the death occurring "on their watch"---creating feelings of anger, guilt, and horrible failure. The parents believe that they were responsible for protecting the child with some control over the child's future—and now the child is no more. Everyone realizes that life tragedies will occur beyond one's control. However, to the mourning parents, that realization might not be comfortable or acceptable. The "soul hurt" is greater than the realization.

If the child chooses to end his or her life through suicidal means, the parent may experience guilt and anger, especially if no note was left. The parent and siblings can be possessed with the "shoulds" for a long duration:

"I should have seen the symptoms."
"Why wasn't a note left?"
"What should I have done?"

These thoughts will never be answered which can create extreme frustration and intense guilt.

When the child dies before the parents, the supportive individuals need to be understanding and accepting of the raw emotions coming from all of the family members. There are no easy answers. There should be no condemnation of the family's emotions. No judgments should be made....just lots of love, nurturing, and understanding.

9

Death and the Funeral

After the shock and denial of the death of a loved one, the survivors are vulnerable to yet another series of emotional trials, and that is the funeral arrangements and the funeral. Most of the survivors are probably still dealing with the shock of the death, so when they are dealing with the funeral arrangements, they may not remember what was actually said. Their physical body may be in attendance, but their mental and emotional alertness and awareness are farmed out in their psyche. It is wise to take a friend to listen in on the funeral arrangements.

It is not uncommon for some of the bereaved, at a later date, to ask someone what the funeral was like. *"Who was there?" "What did the speakers say about the deceased one?" "How did he or she get to the grave site ceremony?" "What was the most moving part of the funeral service?"*

The funeral is the means in which we realize that finality has occurred. It offers the loved ones a chance to say their final good-byes to the physical body.

***Many bereaved people find the funeral is a turning point
where the full reality of the death hits directly home.***
—Dr. Beverley Raphael

Throughout the funeral service, a bereaved person may be able to come to terms of the significant loss. It may occur during the music, or happen while the individuals are speaking, or during the quiet moments of silence.

Some funeral services permit people in attendance to express their grief and loss accompanying the death. They become active participants in the service, and that feels good to those who are going through the bereavement. The funeral can be of the nature of celebrating the life of the deceased. The opportunity presents itself for friends and family to come together for personal support in dealing with the beloved one's demise. The emotional, mental, social, spiritual, and physical support helps the bereaved persons to maneuver through the first stages of bereavement.

The funeral is not as much for the deceased as it is for the family and friends. It is a time to show love, to express concern, to say good-bye, and to feel even closer to the family members who are left. Someone might want to put an object in the casket, such as a toy, ring, or even a baseball. Some visitors will not overtly show any mourning or emotion and that too is normal. There is no "One Way" to show our sadness. Each of us is different and based on our traditions, life experiences, and personal relationships, we view life and death from our own perspective, and not from another person's.

No one is ever really prepared for the death of someone loved.
—Alan Wolfelt

Funerals are primarily for the family, not for friends or spectators. The family needs private time together to express their individual good-byes. They are gathered to pay tribute to the lossed one. They need the freedom to express their grief, by talking out their feelings and thoughts, by recalling favorite memories, by shedding sorrowful tears, by reading a poem honoring the life of the deceased, by surrounding the casket and singing the person's favorite songs, or even laughing about the deceased's idiosyncrasies. Each of these are normal, natural, and perhaps needed. All of these are possibilities depending on the wishes of the survivors.

Our rational self realizes that only the physical body/shell/cocoon is still left. Many believe that the person's spirit is alive and has made the transition into another state of being. However, our emotional self may not find such rational thoughts comfortable or acceptable. At the time of the funeral, the survivors may not have peace of mind about such a transition.

The family members should have the option on whether they wish to be a part of planning the funeral and grave site service. Some will desire to do so while others may not be comfortable in such a situation.

For those who wish to be an integral part of the funeral details, they should have the opportunity to be involved on every level of each decision. It isn't designed to be a "one man show" making all the decisions. By doing so, it can create resentment, sorrow, and "being left out" of a very important ceremony.

Because we are hurting intensely, we sometimes give the reins to complete strangers to do the major funeral arrangements. We become the spectators! This can cause serious repercussions if the funeral planning turned out not to be to our personal "liking" during the funeral and grave site services.

As survivors, we have the right to not be a spectator at our loved one's funeral. After all, we certainly know what our loved one would wish rather than what a stranger would know. Dealing with the grief over a loved one is painfully slow, very difficult at times, and can wear out a griever. Funeral arrangements are not easy and are not meant to be because the survivor is dealing with the loss of a loved one. Sometimes the grief and sorrow seem like they will never end. It takes diligent work to move through the grief to the brighter side of total acceptance. One cannot move successfully through grief without also experiencing legitimate, genuine growth. One follows the other: **pain creates growth**.

One of the tragedies in our society's culture is that we believe we need to tranquilize those who are having a difficult experience at the funeral or grave site. This is a huge error of judgment. The medication covers up the pain we are legitimately experiencing and camouflages the pain and sorrow.

If there is a wide gulf between your faith and feelings right now because of the hurt and pain you are feeling, that's not hypocrisy—that's honesty.
---Joey O'Connor

If we do not actualize the loss, making it real, and owning it, then the intense grief remains unresolved! Such is a personal disaster, a time bomb, ready at the **BOOM!** The boom will create insurmountable personal destructive, unbelievable horror, and prolonged depression, hurt, and helplessness.

What some families in our culture do is to not hold funeral services but rather Celebration of Life services. It focuses not on the death of the individual but rather on the fun and glory of the deceased individual. Friends are urged and encouraged to attend the Celebration.

The Celebration is usually marked with positive affirmations and "mature" laughter from the speakers and the audience. It can be a refreshing service, focusing on the positive and not on the negative. During the Celebration service, the bereaved may wish to have a memorial service in which individuals pay homage to the deceased. It is a wonderful way for people to say good-bye and to allow them an opportunity to express heart-felt sentiments.

The death becomes real as family members and friends remember the life of the loved one. The individuals can begin to face their grief and to start their journey of recovery.

Because it is a celebration of one's life, the family may wish to remember their loved one in a tangible way. Planting a tree, establishing scholarships, preparing a memorial garden, or releasing balloons each year on the loved one's birthday can be a marvelous way to celebrate a life that was loving, meaningful, remarkable, and of course, valuable.

Many individuals have planned the details of their personal funeral or Celebration Service. There is nothing morbid about doing this. Individuals want specific things to be done and other things not done. They may wish certain music to be played, specific speakers, the type of service, the passage of Scripture, and even the pallbearers.

Life is lived forward but understood backward.
—Kierkegaard

10

The Love of a Friend

"What can I do for those who are going through the grieving process?"
"Am I needed?"
"What do they need?"

When a loved one passes on, friends can be a tremendous means of helping to ease the emotional pain. Their empathy pours into the hurt souls of those who are left behind. While family members are locked into their grieving, they are in great need of support and love. The most difficult time of a person's grieving is when all of the friends have paid their sincere respects and resumed their lives. The mourning family is now alone and still lost in an emotional fog. Many of the supporters are no longer accessible to assist with the needs of the family. Sadly, it is at this time when a "life rope" needs to be available to each person in the grieving family. It may be that these individuals require help even months after the funeral ceremony. The hearts of the survivors are in pieces, and their souls are bruised.

For one reason or another, some individuals are highly nervous when talking about death or being around those who are experiencing a death. They become uneasy, avoiding the subject of death. The bereaved can at times be treated by others as if something, like death, is unnatural and foreign.

Due to such uneasy behavior, a person's tongue and brain might get twisted. They may express awkward statements, such as *"I thought*

61

you'd be okay by now," or *"It's been five days since the funeral, so how are you doing?"* To the bereaved, *"How are you doing"* is like asking, *"How was the play, Mrs. Lincoln?"* The bereaved can still be stunned about the dynamics surrounding the death. If a person has yet to face a significant death, he or she may feel ill-at-ease saying an appropriate expression, such as *"I'm praying for your family,"* or *"Please know you are in my thoughts."* Sometimes no words need to be said...just a brief hug will do.

We have good intentions, and we want to aid the survivors. There are many actions that friends and relatives can do.

RESPOND IMMEDIATELY

When we first hear of the bereaved facing the death of a loved one, we need to get to the scene of where they are. They may be at home or the hospital. If we are geographically close, we are able to respond quickly. If we are far away, a phone call to the bereaved can be done. Phone call—no texts, no e-mails because they are a poor way of sending one's sentiments. If traveling to the scene is impossible, a phone call is second best.

Whatever the means, we need to get in touch with the bereaved. The survivors will be indebted to us because our contact means we care. We can sense their pain and hurt.

MAKE YOUR PRESENCE KNOWN

This is important because the bereaved needs to know that the supportive person is present and available. The grieving individuals may need things done that the supportive individual can handle. The person may be the "gopher" who runs errands or makes necessary phone calls or tackles the home needs, such as vacuuming, washing clothes, or preparing the meals.

There was an elderly gentleman who was an acquaintance of the family living several blocks away. When one of the family's children died in a boating accident, the community turned out in full force as well as the elderly man. Their home was filled with sympathizers. The elderly gentleman was welcomed into the home and quickly forgotten. As the hours passed, the community folks gradually left—except for the kind old man. When the grieving parents realized that he was still somewhere in the house, they went looking for him. They found him upstairs, sitting on the floor, surrounded by the shoes belonging to the family. He was polishing each one of them. The grieving father spoke first. *"Sir, what are you doing?"* The gentleman, with a sparkle in his eyes, responded. *"Well, I knew you would want to look your best at the funeral tomorrow, so I decided that the best thing that I could do for your family is to polish your shoes."* The parents broke down and wept over his kindness and thoughtfulness.

From time to time during the visit, it is appropriate to express one's love for the bereaved. It does not have to be in words. Just a simple word or a hug can work.

AVOID CLICHES

We might not need to use cliches, but at times, they are expressed. The following cliches need to be avoided:

"She is in a better place."
"It was God's will."
"At least you can have other children."
"Time heals all pain."
"I'm sure she is happy now."
"It's for the best."
"God works in mysterious ways."
"Eventually you'll get over it."
"You'll get to see your loved one again one day."
"God needed a perfect angel and now He has one."
"Something better will come along."
"You need to pull yourself up by the bootstraps and get on with life."
"May your loved one rest in peace."

A simple *"I'm sorry,"* or *"I'm here for you"* can work just fine. Breaking one's neck to express a highfalutin comment can find our foot in our well-meaning mouth.

ALLOW EMOTIONS TO FLOW

The bereaved has stepped outside of her or his natural self and has become a person in shock. The bereaved will need the love and comfort of the supportive person to cry out a barrage of emotional feelings: denial, guilt, anger, and sadness.

The supportive person needs to encourage and to allow any and all feelings to flow freely. There should not be any barriers placed on the tongue of the bereaved. If we really wish to help the bereaved, then we should listen intently and speak little. We are not to conduct counseling sessions. We are there to be what the bereaved wants. Being a supportive individual is an honor which has varied responsibilities, if done correctly.

There will be times when the bereaved will be irrational in expressing one's thoughts and feelings. This is normal and natural. The supportive person is not with the bereaved to judge the person's thoughts and emotions. More than likely, the bereaved has no intention of carrying through with the irrational thoughts. The bereaved is striking out at death and at the world as a result of the death.

Before leaving the bereaved to return home, the supportive person can further help the survivor by leaving notes of encouragement in the rooms that the bereaved is sure to use.

REMAIN IN CONTACT LONG AFTER THE LOSS

When the funeral is over, the friends and relatives usually return to their homes. The bereaved person is left sadly alone. The nights become long and lonely. It is after the funeral that many bereaved ones need a supportive person on hand. Weeks and months pass, and some bereaved seldom hear from anyone. After the funeral is over, this may be the time when the bereaved begins ranting at a full degree. It is very important that supportive individuals remain in contact with the bereaved, even months after the loss. There will come a time when the bereaved is ready to "step outside" into society once again and will need help. This is when the supportive person can be of great assistance to the bereaved one.

———

As long as the memory of certain beloved friends
lives in my heart, I shall say life is good.
—Helen Keller

———

Not all people will be able to identify with a survivor because they have yet to lose a significant person in their lives. And others may not have the mental and emotional foundation to integrate into the mentality and emotions of the bereaved. It indeed takes a special person to be able to identify with the varied feelings that a survivor is encountering. Even if the special person has not experienced a significant death yet, the person has developed an inner spirit that can understand and feel the hurt and sorrow within the bereaving individual by simply listening and being accessible.

The special person(s) have developed the sense of empathy. They are like a magnet. They can draw people to them because they can sense that individuals can safely relate thoughts and emotions—with unconditional acceptance, no judgments, and no strings attached to the relationship. The special ones send out vibrations that they can be trusted which permits them to be genuine and honest. They can be a "walking and talking" miracle to those who are dealing with a significant death.

An empathetic individual can "feel" the pain, the hurt, and the traumatic suffering that is continually occupying the life of the survivor. An empathetic person doesn't have to carry on a conversation with the bereaved. Simply being in the presence of the bereaved can be enough at that moment. The empathetic individual knows from deep within when to talk versus when not to. Such an individual realizes that the bereaved has "bruises" on his or her soul. The bruises may be guilt, shame, anger, despair, and depression. The individual with empathy can be a vibrant part of placing ointment on the bruises by attentive listening and at specific times, verbally by communicating with the bereaved one. It is as if the empathetic individual has a heightened sensitivity within oneself. Such sensitivity allows the person to "walk in the shoes" of the survivor. The empathetic individual can "feel" the immense hurt of the bereaved. As a result, the empathetic person is on top of everything that the bereaved may be possibly thinking and feeling.

The individual with an empathetic personality is a life-savor to the multitude of bereaved who are struggling to make it through the day-at-hand. The bereaved person is burdened down with not only the specific death but also with all the outward dynamics surrounding the loss, such as role responsibilities, other family members with their emotions, funeral obligations, and workplace responsibilities. The sadness of hopelessness and helplessness can put the bereaved on the very edge of life.

The empathetic person can "read" into all of these conflicts facing the survivor(s). The loving friend asks for no praise, compliment, or glorification. The person gives freely of oneself because being empathetic is who they are.

The empathetic individual needs to hear the raw emotions of the bereaved in order to attempt to identify with the inner struggles of the survivor. In doing so, he or she offers support and continual encouragement. They, in a sense, become our life cheerleaders. The empatheic listener helps the bereaved to struggle out of the depressive cave into the sunshine as the bereaved battles against the ever-present stress and horrendous pressures.

One of the loneliest feelings of the survivor is when he or she is in the midst of a death circumstance and believes that no one understands the hurt and that they are totally alone on a mysterious, forsaken, uncharted island.

The caring friend: a soothing and kind voice, a soft touch, an empathic countenance. These qualities can help ease the bereaved's internal stormy sea when turmoil and prevailing stressors are devastating and destroying one's inner peace.

Such is the love of a friend.

11

The Grieving Process

Because grief follows the loss of a loved one, grief is universal. Each person does his or her individual mourning because we grieve differently. Whether it is sudden or expected, the loss takes away the presence of a valued loved one. Such grief carries intense emotional pain, and that is inevitable. The severity of the pain is in direct proportion to the degree of importance that the loved one had in our life.

What all of us do know is that a process called grieving is waiting for us once a loved one is absent from us by way of death. If we are ever to accept the loss of our loved one and eventually move on in life, then immersing ourselves into the grief process is a necessity.

While each person will handle the grieving process differently, there is no exact, identical sequence of the grief phases for every person; some stages presented may be reversed, while others may coexist.

Shock and Denial

While it is a huge benefit to have a competent, enduring support system consisting of family members, friends, and professionals to help through the different stages of grief, we carry our grief on a lonely journey.

Whether the loss of one's beloved is sudden or expected, the individual will encounter the news with shock—the beginning stage of the grieving process. It lasts until the person has the capability of moving into the next stage. No matter how emotionally strong a person may appear in everyday routines, shock neutralizes all rational thinking and decision-making.

As a result of the shock, an individual may display some form of emotional release. This release may be weeping, screaming, acting aggressively, laughing nervously, or pacing. Each person will deal with the type of release in his or her own way, which may be totally different from the ways of others going through the same loss. Whatever means a person chooses, that individual has the right to allow his or her emotions and behavior to be freely expressed in any time and in any place.

Repressing one's feelings, in addition to the shock itself, can have serious repercussions, such as physical and psycho-physiological ailments. The physical ailments can be a loss of appetite, a lack of muscular power, insomnia, or tightness in the throat. The psycho-physiological results might be ulcers, hypertension, or aggressive acts of behavior. These repercussions might not surface for quite some time after the loss. However, if the grieving person is free to ventilate the feelings of anguish, then the repercussions may not occur—or if they do, the intensity might be lessened.

As the shock wears off, and after the initial emotional releases have occurred, the mourning person then faces additional stages of grief. The healthier individual will emerge as the one who faces the grief stages without repressing the involved feelings. The individual who suppresses the genuine feelings only postpones the inevitable—dealing with the shock of the grief at a later date.

The emotion of shock carries with it many feelings that the bereaved cannot possibly deal with all at the same time. The emotions operate on their own timetable and will present themselves whenever and wherever. Depending upon the griever's personality and the relationship between the loss and the griever, the shock will vary in its duration. The griever needs to permit whatever emotions the shock dictates. This is normal, healthy, and necessary.

> *The fear of death follows from the fear of life. A man*
> *who lives fully is prepared to die at any time.*
> —Mark Twain

When the terrible shock lessens, which can occur hours or days after the news of the loss, the loved ones may then come face-to-face with the devastating loss: *"I just saw Mark yesterday. He never said he was feeling bad." "Barbara saw the doctor two days ago. No way could she have had a stroke." "Tim and Carol watched little Chip like a hawk. How could he have drowned in their pool? I refuse to believe that he is really dead!"*

Once the shock is over, the denial of the situation begins. The news comes with a resounding **boom!** We are left stunned—almost speechless. The shock stage is intermingled with denial. We may not even know when one starts and the other finishes.

STAGE ONE
Existing in Denial Keeps the Individual in Neutral Gear

Denial can be a defense mechanism that acts as a mental and emotional safeguard. As a result of remaining in denial, an individual becomes like a zombie living in human clothing. Even those who are surrounding the mortified individual with concern and compassion may find getting through to the individual an impossibility. Until the bereaved is ready and prepared to move out of the denial stage, it becomes a waiting game.

Denial is the stage in which we can collect ourselves after the shock and emerge out of the murky waters that we were not prepared for. Denial becomes our rescue in a world of turmoil and chaos. When a grieving person is in the midst of denial, the individual may be vaguely aware of the sounds of words from a supportive friend. However, the words are merely registered as sounds by the bereaved because the denial has placed an invisible blockage around the "denial mind."

Denial is a means to temporarily escape from the harsh reality of our loss. The bereaved is not prepared to face the details of life until the denial is an accepted part of the grieving process. The bereaved needs to accept denial as being okay and healthy. When the loss has impacted multiple individuals, the separate individuals will emerge out of denial at different times. In a healthy situation, there will come a time when denial can no longer be maintained. Decisions following a loss must be carried through, and such necessary decision-making may bring the denial to a halt. However, it is possible that the bereaved may make the needed decisions while still in denial. The bereaved may go through the motions of acting normal while still existing in the denial state. The bereaved is on auto-pilot.

It is not unusual for the bereaved to isolate himself or herself from others during the denial stage. Isolation can be a means of self-preservation; it can be used as a time to hurt, to grieve, to be quiet, to elicit fond memories, to think, to feel, or to simply be left alone in one's own private arena. The individual may wish to isolate himself or herself from everyone else so as not to face comments and questions. Isolation can be a healing balm that enables the bereaved to continue to the next stage in the grieving process. The isolation should not alarm the ones making up the support system; it needs to be respected.

For those who are involved with the mourning individual during the isolation phase, it is important to continue a presence with the bereaved. Out of respect for the isolated bereaved, don't force conversations or push the bereaved to get "with the living" by going places. The bereaved may need uninterrupted quietness—silent nonverbal communication. It can have redeeming results. It is up to the bereaved to decide when conversations should be started or when facing the public is warranted. Sometimes the whole realm of isolation bothers the support group more than it does the bereaved.

STAGE TWO
Anger: A Volatile Emotion

The most powerful, most volatile emotion we have is anger. There is absolutely nothing wrong with having anger. What does make it dangerous is what we do with it. When it causes us to do physical damage, to hurt someone, to destroy, or to seek revenge, then anger assumes the dark side of our personality. On the other hand, when anger is used to correct a wrong, to protect others, or to defend oneself in a nonviolent way, then it can be a useful tool.

Anger is an emotion that occurs in a majority of grieving individuals. Depending on a person's make up and the circumstances involving that person's loss, anger will be demonstrated in various forms. It may range from simple to violent outbursts, from sedate tears to lashing out, or from silence to uncontrollable screaming.

The grief stage of anger is complex. The reason for that is that anger is multidirectional. The mourner can become angry at life or at the loss, and the anger might be directed at preachers, doctors, nurses, friends, family members, or even God: *"How could you let this happen, God, after all the prayers I made?" "God, I've tried to be the best person I can, and you do this to me?" "So, God, do you have any other surprises?"* There is nothing—absolutely nothing—wrong about being angry—again, it's what one does with it.

The anger can be overtly directional through outbursts of temper, irrational behavior, and hostile behavior. On the other hand, an even worse thing is when the anger is internalized and never dealt with. When the bereaved turns the anger inward, he or she may place tremendous blame on himself or herself for not being able to supernaturally prevent the loss. Furthermore, suppressing the anger will definitely cause that anger to show itself later in horrific ways. Unresolved, suppressed anger can be a time bomb just waiting to explode anytime and anywhere, at anyone.

Anger can transform the griever into a human monster until the wrath is resolved. While the mourner may blame everyone connected with the loss, there is really no one person directly responsible. However, the anger of the bereaved may become increasingly intensified. This blame opens wide the internal door of guilt. This torturous thinking can create an inner volcano of angry feelings that may explode at various times in the mourning period, or even years later.

In dealing with anger, the bereaved has a battle both externally and internally. Because anger is such a powerful emotion, it has the potential to turn the griever into a person who is not recognizable to himself or herself, or to others. The pain of the bereaved hurts so much that no one may be exempt from the rage. As the hurt continues, the anger can become increasingly strengthened. The griever is likely to be irrational at times, verbalizing the anger even at individuals who are no longer part of the person's life: *"How dare you leave me all alone. What am I supposed to do now?" "Why did you stop being my friend? I need you now."*

⟜

Everyone is handed adversity in life. No one's journey is easy. It's how they handle it that makes people unique.
—Kevin Conroy

⟜

Having anger during the mourning stages is normal, expected, and natural. As a person allows the angry feelings to manifest toward others, the bereaved seldom intends the hostile feelings to be taken personally. The bereaved is in deep pain. Therefore, the individual to whom the anger is directed is not the real enemy. The real anger is at the loss, not the people surrounding it.

Like a cluster of grapes, anger has several emotions attached to it. Each grape in the cluster represents a separate gut-wrenching feeling: guilt, depression, denial, vindictiveness, hopelessness, helplessness, self-pity, and loneliness. When dealing with each of these emotional reactions, in addition to the raw anger, the longevity of one's healing journey cannot be realistically predicted. However, anger can be lessened when the griever vents the feelings in an open and honest manner without being embarrassed, guilty, or ashamed.

STAGE THREE
Depression: A Horrendous Nightmare

Clinical depression is an illness. It is debilitating! At some time in the progression of grief, the bereaved may suffer from some form of depression, which can range from temporary sadness to bona fide clinical depression. It will have a vicious impact on the bereaved. This monstrous illness will steal one's ability to enjoy life's activities: going to fun places, exercising, being outdoors, planting a garden, being with friends—all of these and many more. It traps the victim behind an invisible wall. The depressed individual can become not only emotionally paralyzed but also physically unable to deal with daily responsibilities. Depression can occur in adults, teenagers, and children. Individuals in all of these age groups may be impacted by the loss of a loved one.

A grieving, depressed person may feel that one can never fill the empty space that the loss has left. The person's whole world has seemingly split apart, and there doesn't appear to be any sense to life. Because of intense despair, the individual, therefore, may experience the horrors of clinical depression. A search for meaning in life becomes futile.

It is not length of life, but depth of life.
—Waldo Emerson

Each of us will encounter someone who is suffering from depression while that person is involved in the grieving process. It might not be a pretty sight. We want to help the person but are not certain how. We can indeed feel helpless when this situation arises.

There has to be a clear understanding between genuine sadness over the loss of a person in one's life and clinical depression. Friends who have lost an individual may feel sad and heart-broken without necessarily suffering from clinical depression. Severe depression can impact those who had an intimate relationship with the loved one. Those family members and close friends of their beloved may feel that the special empty space left behind will never be filled. Nothing can fill such shoes—fun, laughter, a silly sense of humor, a unique sense of compassion, undying love, loyalty—the universe of the bereaved has become shreds of despair, confusion, and shock.

For those suffering from depression, there doesn't appear to be any reasonable, rational sense to their purpose on earth any longer. Because the depths of depression are like a bottomless pit, the bereaved may have a tendency to curl up into a fetal position and vegetate. The bereaved is confined in his or her own emotional, mental, and physical prison. Panic and fright are accomplices. The bereaved doesn't know how to break out—or, for that matter, even desires to.

This stage of grief is a resistance to return to the normal activities of life. During the depression, the bereaved may find it difficult, if not impossible, to connect with loved ones. As a result, the mourner isolates himself or herself socially. The grief is too overwhelming. The entire bodily system of the bereaved aches deeply. Being around friends who remind the bereaved of the loss may be traumatic; therefore, the person desires to isolate himself or herself from the hurt.

The depression and the isolation allow the mourner to escape doing daily tasks. Dealing with responsibilities is placed on the back burner for the time being. To the griever, life is no longer pretty, exciting, or fun; it has become mean and ugly. Facing the reality of the loss may seem impossible during this stage of the grieving process. The emotional pain is excruciating as the bereaved finds himself or herself in the throes of depression, isolation, and anger. The mainstream of life will just have to wait.

There is no answer to the question of how long the depression will last. The individuals who make up the support system must be patient and very understanding, with a huge helping of compassion. The bereaved needs love and kindness. Furthermore, it is important to remember that the time line belongs to the one who is in bereavement, not to the individuals who are the support system.

STAGE FOUR
Guilt: A Devastating Emotion

Having the emotion of guilt is not new to any of us. Guilt is an open doorway we have all traveled through at various times in our relationships with family members and friends. The guilt following the loss of a loved one can be mentally and emotionally paralyzing. It carries the weight of self-blame and self-doubt. Concerning a recent loss, a person's mind is occupied with many questions that cannot be answered. But we still seek answers: *"Could I have done anything to prevent the loss?" "What actions could have prevented it?" "Am I at fault?""How can I stop the guilt?" "Does the guilt mean I was at fault?"*

Guilt can be mean. It wars against the conscience, and usually the guilt wins. There seems at times to be no escape from the haunting pattern of guilty thoughts and the horrifying accompanying emotions. In reality the guilt might not be justified, but if the individual believes it is, then the guilt is an invader. The guilty thoughts can result in self-punishing and detrimental behavior, especially if a person feels responsible for a loss because of what was done or not done.

Guilt can be a stronghold in anyone's daily life when it has not been dealt with effectively. As a result, the individual lives a sorrowful, demeaning existence. It keeps the person from having joy, happiness, and mental and emotional freedom. An individual might hold on to guilt tenaciously over actions that occurred years before. They become an albatross around one's neck. Depending on the significance of the mistake made, the guilt may be long lasting. When the guilt is ever-present, the victim is destined for physical and emotional trauma. The human body is not designed to store heavy doses of guilt without paying a huge price, such as migraines, ulcers, stress, unhappiness, and confusion.

Many varied emotions accompany guilt, such as depression, helplessness, bitterness, and hopelessness. Therefore, the griever is dealing not with just one feeling but multiple ones. The stage of guilt wreaks havoc on the survivor. Feelings of guilt create within people unrealistic attitudes and appraisals of not being a grade A family member or friend. As a result, the bereaved chastises himself or herself for missing the mark of being the "perfect" one in the relationship. This self-punishment, plus the guilt reactions, can be devastating. The loved one cannot simply wish away the feeling of guilt. It has to be faced head-on in order to be dealt with successfully.

Life is a balance of holding on and letting go.
—Rumi

The feelings of guilt will not disappear overnight. In her book, Death in the School Community, Martha Oates relates a letter that a fifteen-year-old wrote her brother who had died two years previously.

> *I can't believe you are gone. All I can remember is seeing you in the hospital. It was so hard for me to touch or even look at you. I hurt all over. You knew I loved you and so did Mom and Dad. Maybe I should have told you more often that I loved you. I feel it is my fault. Do you ever think our relationship could have been better? I do...I mean it was good, but I would have liked it to be better. I'm so sorry for never telling you I loved you. I'm glad that I have your looks, that way I always have something to remember you by. I miss you a lot. I miss talking to you about my problems. Life is very different without you!*

When the guilt links up with depression, the result is an all-out internal warfare. The person beats himself or herself up into a shabby-looking creature. When combining guilt and depression regarding the loss of a loved one, the picture is one of total blackness. If the bereaved blames himself or herself for the loss of the loved one, the guilt has an open doorway into his or her soul.

Supportive individuals may be assisting a member of a bereaved family through the stage of guilt while at the same time helping another family member deal with anger. Because we are all different and thus grieve differently, there is no time line in the overall grieving process. Owing to the zigzag patterns each loved one brings to the grief table, the supportive persons may feel pulled in different directions through different time lines by different mourners. It is important to recognize and acknowledge this scenario so that the support group realizes that one family member may be closing in on accepting the loss while another individual in the same family may continue to be in one of the other stages.

STAGE FIVE
Acceptance: Onward and Upward

We human beings center our lives around clocks. Clocks dictate when we rise, when we head for work, when we are at home, when we keep appointments, and when we schedule daily activities. Therefore, we desire to schedule the amount of time it will take to reach the acceptance stage in the grieving process. It is difficult to grasp the concept that the acceptance of a loss may take months, or years. As a result, no two persons can reach the acceptance phase at the same time.

Accepting the loss of a loved one doesn't mean forgetting the relationship with the person. Acceptance means that the grieving individual has reached a point at which the individual knows and accepts the loss, having already dealt with the emotions of guilt, anger, depression, and denial.

The acceptance stage is not synonymous with a happy stage. Acceptance occurs when the grieving person's mind is no longer enduring intense, constant pain. The mind is, therefore, free to understand the dynamics of the grief. The mind now allows the person to face and accept the loss without the sting being constantly perpetuated. The mind assists the emotions in realizing the utter finality of the loss. The enormity of the loss has now been understood and accepted. The grieving individual is prepared to enter the healing stage. It is a time of rebuilding.

In the acceptance phase, the griever begins to return to the functional level that resembles the lifestyle before the loss became an issue. The griever can once more enjoy being with friends and taking part in leisure activities. Life has a meaning for him or her once again.

Even when the grieving person has reached the acceptance stage of grief, there will be occasions when mini-grief episodes might occur, such as on holidays, on birthdays, or during special activities. This setback of grief is absolutely normal and expected.

Once one's emotional and mental pain begins to fade and rational thinking processes start once again, the acceptance of the loss may well be in the works. However, even once the acceptance has finally happened, a mourning individual may still have bouts of sadness and grief from time-to-time.

∽

Life is very short. What we have to do must be done in the now.
—Audre Lord

∽

12

The Journey to Recovery

Recovering from the death of a loved one can be a lonely journey even when surrounded by family members and friends. The tedious journey is outward as well as internal. The outward experience deals with the funeral, the grave site service, the notes to be written, the legal matters, the household tasks, and even returning to the workplace. As a close friend told me: *"The grief process at times may have to be packed up in my suitcase and carried with me because of all the things that have to be done."*

The internal journey involves dealing with the emotional trauma, the emotional feelings, the complex mental thoughts, and moving through the grieving process.

During the recovery time, it is impossible to predict how one will feel from day-to-day. On any given day, one may experience grief reactions of restlessness, anxiety, helplessness, confusion, fear, and hopelessness. While all of these are normal reactions, they have the capacity to hurt deeply. At the time, they are real and vibrant. They have the power to incapacitate the grieving individuals for hours, even days. The individual may be so preoccupied with the memories of the deceased that the hurt and despair are too overwhelming. The griever "lives" in the depths of quiet desperation.

When death took my parents, I lost the most significant people in my life. I tried to wrap my mind around the loss. However, no matter how I tried to accept such a death, I couldn't. Everywhere I looked, I would see something that would bring forth wonderful memories of them—places we had gone together, conversations we had, and laughs.

My tears are the words with which I tell God of my pain.
—Adolfo Quezada

The deaths that we face in life may have been our spouse, our child, or a close friend. At times we might feel as if we are in a cloudy maze. The person's memory seems to be encompassing us. We know that our loved one has departed, but our feelings of sorrow and "lostness" are not co-operating with our thoughts. On and on and on we go—we've not had a decent amount of sleep or rest since the dreadful death.

We try our best to handle our grief process, but the shock and denial are much too powerful to proceed. Too hurtful. Too sad. We can't see any light at this point.

When we are able to travel down the grieving process, we long at times for a break—a little release from the pain. We know the bereavement process will take time—sometimes a lot of time. We seek to cry out our tears to ease our tension, stress, and heartache.

There is no embarrassment regarding crying in public or in private. We have lost a significant person in our life, and our world will never be quite the same again.

There were many times that I reached for the phone to call my parents, only to quickly realize that neither was here any longer. They had been my bulwark in life, never failing to be available whenever I wished. My dad and mom were the ultimate cheerleaders who never tired out. They were my clowns who could make me laugh. And they were my confidants who protected my privacy.

It is not unusual to be angry over the death of our significant person. The harshness can be directed at God, at nurses, at doctors, or even at other family members. It also is not unusual to become angry at the person for dying: *"Why did you leave me?" "How do you expect me to go on?"* The anger can be irrational—it doesn't have to make sense. We owe ourselves no apology or guilt for being angry. The emotions belong to us, and there is no right or wrong to it. "It" is responding to our sorrow.

There will be days when we barely can get through the day. We might be able to take one hour at a time, and that is all we can do. The list of tasks we wanted to accomplish by the end of the day does not become a reality. If the grief is overwhelming on a particular day, we just might get only **one** task done. This is normal, natural, and expected. Being good to oneself means erasing all of our expectations for the day and concentrating on living an hour at a time.

While the griever is experiencing the psychological grief reactions, he or she can also be plagued with the physical problems of extreme fatigue, spells of intense crying, loss of sleep, heart palpitations, panic attacks, and a drastic change in one's appetite. While these are normal, the griever may not feel normal.

Grief is hard work, and accepting the death of a loved one does not take place overnight. One's health becomes vulnerable to illnesses. Thus, it is vital that the grieving individual maintain one's health:

- Eating the proper food. (Living on jello and popcorn is not the answer)
- Adequate sleep and rest. Naps are healthy. Resting during the day is essential. Watch television, call a friend, read a magazine or book, play with your pet, take a short walk.

Helping to heal one's broken heart can be accomplished by close friends or family members. These supportive individuals can do many acts of kindness which will lessen the grief at the time:

- Go on short walks with the bereaved.
- Listen to the thoughts and feelings of the griever.

- Do household chores for the person.
- Run errands.
- Answer the telephone.
- Express encouraging words.

Because we miss our loved one so very much, we make the mistake of making "big" decisions immediately after the death, such as moving to another location, changing the familiar furniture, or removing the beloved's clothes. All of these can eventually be accomplished if they remain on our "to do" list. However, it is prudent to postpone such decisions for six to eight months after the death. If not, then the survivor may regret acting too hastily.

When an entire family system is impacted by a death in the family, the grieving is paramount. No one can be the "strong" one to take charge because that particular individual is also grieving intensely. Everyone is going through devastation. If a grieving person "hides" behind the role of the "strong" one, that person will inevitably have to come to grips with the death in the future. And the support group may no longer be present or accessible. This can become a horrible reality. A grieving individual has the right to mourn like the other members without thinking or feeling he or she has to be the "deliverance" spokesperson for the rest of the grieving family members.

Even if we have tangled with grief before,
this new grief may be different.
—Harold Ivan Smith

It is not unusual at all for those affected by the death to enter in a daze for days following the death. One's mind seems to go into oblivion. The stupor permits the individual to fully acknowledge the death and to move eventually into the details of the final good-byes, and to "own" that a death has actually occurred. At the time while we are in a daze, we become mechanical in our chores, such as preparing a meal, cleaning the laundry, or even walking the dog. We are still in a fog while conducting everyday tasks that are manageable.

Our home becomes cold, quiet, empty, and lonely even in the presence of our supportive individuals. Again, this is normal and in time, the grief will lessen its intensity. All of the family members should be actively included in the dying process and in the funeral arrangements. It is healthy if the survivors wish to dispel the "cold, quiet" home with memorable stories about the deceased. The recollections can both be serious and humorous. This can take the "chill" off the home.

As each member of the family shares experiences that they had with the deceased individual, healthy and honest feelings present themselves. There develops a marvelous communication among the family which helps in the healing process.

I thank my God upon every remembrance of you.
—Philippians 1:3

Prayer is a means of finding strength and peace. What one sees on the outside does not match what is going on inside, because the bereaved individual is grief-stricken beyond one's wildest imagination. The survivor can feel solace in a spiritual sense. A common prayer is to ask God for a miracle when one is dealing with a loved one's illness. We ask God to show us a miracle, and He does. God's miracles are in human form. The miracle may be a pastor who offers soothing and encouraging words or a hospice nurse who gives medical assistance and advice, or a social worker who is qualified to assist in legal ways. A professional counselor is a miracle from God—a counselor who listens intently to our hurt, accepts unconditionally our anguished feelings, and understands what we must be enduring. Even the neighbor who cooks the meals and runs the errands is God's gift to the bereaved—God's miracle. Being human, we would like for God to "heal" our loved one of the illness, but God does not always work that way. However, He does send us miracles in the form of human beings.

God gives us memories so we might have roses in December.
—Marilyn Heavilin

Because grief is a process, and not just an event, God will continue to send His miracles—your answer to your prayers.

There is a tendency to return to normal activities much too soon. The bereaved may not give oneself enough time to get acquainted to the "new Normal" without one's loved one. The person's mind may not have had time to wrap itself around the death or the situation causing the death. The emotional pain cannot be erased, but it can be eased as the survivor begins to accept that a death has occurred.

The bereaved may wish to talk about the deceased. Avoidance of letting that happen by friends and family members can be hurtful to the bereaved individuals. They may wish to acknowledge the very existence of the loved one—to keep the memory of the person alive. The bereaved will set the pace. If it is too hurtful still to talk about the loved one, the bereaved will certainly let you know by words or facial expressions.

It is difficult for the bereaved to be compassionate to oneself along the grief journey. However, it is essential. The bereaved needs to be good to self if healing is to occur. When the bereaved wants to be in seclusion, it should be honored by the supportive individuals. On the other hand, the bereaved may wish to be surrounded by just a few friends. Whatever the bereaved wishes, within reason, should be encouraged and respected. Helping such a person means being sensitive to his or her needs. This permits the survivor to have compassion and patience on oneself.

It is during the time of seclusion that the bereaved may wish to caress the deceased's clothes, and even savor the smell. This can help the healing process. Besides the clothes, the bereaved may look at the deceased's jewelry because he or she can still remember what the loved one looked like when wearing it.

Perhaps the loved one was reading a book but had not finished it. The survivor may want to finish it in memory of the deceased. It is not unusual for the bereaved to save a lock of hair of the deceased. It is during this time of quietness and lonesomeness that the survivor wishes to touch it or hold it close to oneself. Listening to the favorite music of the deceased can have a soothing effect. The healing process requires cooperation from the supportive people with the desires of the bereaved. Under no circumstances can the grief process be rushed. It is like a slow moving stream, finally flowing to its destination. The survivor may wish to have a memorial ceremony with just a few friends. This is an opportunity for the bereaved and close friends to start a scrapbook, featuring the loved one. In this way, each person can express outwardly his or her feelings and thoughts.

When the bereaved is ready, one can keep a journal of the life of the deceased, plus writing down one's thoughts and emotions. The journal will be a wonderful treasure that will be everlasting. Before the ill loved one dies, the survivor may want to record the person's voice. This takes away the fear that one will forget in time what the person sounded like.

It is not unusual for the survivor to feel "stuck" after the grieving process is finished. An important person is now absent. There is a tremendous vacancy—a hole—an emptiness. In order to deal with these feelings, the survivor must begin a "new life" without the loved one.

Even if your hold on God seems to slip at times—
don't worry. God has a firm hold on you!
—David Paap

Beginning a new hobby is an excellent means of dealing with one's grieving emotions. The hobby becomes a new activity on which to focus. Besides a new hobby, the survivor may need to restore and to energize oneself by engaging in outdoor activities, such as camping, hiking, gardening, bike riding, or simply strolling around the neighborhood. When the time is right, a bereaved person can shift one's attention from oneself to become a part-time volunteer at a school, nursing home, hospital, or community center.

Whatever the survivor decides to do, it is not dishonoring the memory of the loved one. It can be a healing ointment for the soul of the survivor. When a loved one dies, life seems to become more complex and stressful. The grieving person may need to simplify life-in-general by cutting out "stuff" of no importance. There are things in our lives that were once considered necessary and vital. However, upon closer evaluation, a person may see that some things are not as important, especially after the reality of the death becomes very real. Simplifying "life" reduces stress and anxiety, and therefore life becomes more manageable. Simply say NO to things you don't want to do until later on.

Everyone who has experienced a significant death can use a "grief friend" to talk with. The friend realizes that the bereaved is hurting, and the friend is willing to listen attentively. We may want to talk about our loved one and the wonderful memories we have. On the other hand, we may need to talk about the grief we are enduring. It is very important to communicate our thoughts and feelings to a trusted individual, whether it be our spouse or a close relative or a friend. Getting the feelings out in the open allows us to handle them better than to keep them enclosed in our mental vault. Rather than visiting the grave on one's own, taking a loved one with you can at times be easier and perhaps more comfortable. It may be painful at times to visit the grave site, but the pain must be experienced for healing.

The bereaved is usually surrounded by family members and friends at the onset of the grieving journey (denial stage), and the bereaved can use the attention. However, there will be times when the bereaved needs solitude to process what has happened. In addition, the time alone can be spent reflecting on the memories that he or she has of the one who is no longer. The bereaved may wish to go alone on a walk or read notes the deceased wrote while in the relationship. During this time the bereaved will have the chance to embrace alone the flood of emotions. If the bereaved doesn't "own" the feelings and deal with them effectively, healing cannot take place. Having memories of the loved one may stir specific positive and negative feelings that the bereaved must honor and process. This at times requires solitude. The bereaved might wish to create a "prayer room" which is furnished and reserved only for the bereaved individual. The room becomes a safe haven where it is quiet and conducive for thought and emotional processing.

The supporters need to respect the **DO NOT DISTURB** look and actions of the bereaved. The bereaved person decides when and if they wish to express the deep pain inhabiting their body and mind.

The caregiver needs to simply walk alongside of the bereaved, to go where the path leads, and for as long as the journey takes.
—Kenneth Doka

The caregivers need to grant permission, so to speak, to the bereaved to show his or her emotions, no matter if positive or negative. In this way, the bereaved is not left alone with the overwhelming feelings.

The caregivers may suggest to the bereaved to keep a journal. In it, the bereaved can write his or her thoughts and feelings about the death and its aftermath. The bereaved may find that writing down the emotions and thoughts is far easier than expressing them vocally.

Since the grief is personal and painstaking at the same time, the bereaved does not need to be the "strong" one. The grief may be so intense and hurtful that being the strong one is just about impossible. The role of the strong one can be designated to a caregiver. The caregiver can make the rational decisions and follow through on what actions need doing.

Recovering from a loved one's death may be a long journey for some individuals, which is okay. The bereaved is traveling down a long road... alone. Therefore, the journey with its twists, turns and detours must be honored, respected, and accepted by the faithful caregivers who can encourage the bereaved and remain close-at-hand.

THE MOURNER'S CODE

1. You have the right to experience your own unique grief.
2. You have the right to talk about your grief.
3. You have the right to feel a multitude of emotions.
4. You have the right to be tolerant of your physical & emotional limits.
5. You have the right to experience "griefbursts".
6. You have the right to make use of ritual.
7. You have the right to embrace your spirituality.
8. You have the right to search for meaning.
9. You have the right to treasure your memories.
10. You have the right to move toward your grief & heal.

—Alan D. Wolfelt
Healing the Adult Child's Grieving Heart.

━━◆

When death takes away those we love most, then we really learn about just how short our time on earth is and why what we do with that time matters.
—James Comey
A Higher Loyalty

━━◆

Bibliography

Akner, Lois F. How to survive the loss of a parent. New York: William Morrow & company, 1993.

Doka, Kenneth & Joyce Davidson (eds). Living with grief: who we are, how we grieve. Hospice Foundation of America, 1998.

Heavilin, Marilyn Willett. Roses in december. Eugene, Oregon: Harvest House Publishers, 1987.

Kubler-Ross, Elisabeth. On death and dying. New York: Macmillan Publishing Co., 1969.

Kubler-Ross, Elisabeth. On children and death. New York: Macmillan Publishing Co., 1983.

Levy, Alexander. The orphaned adult. Cambridge: Perseus Publishing, 1999.

Myers, Edward. When parents die. New York: Penquin, 1986.

Oates, Martha. Death in the school community. Alexandria, Va: American Counseling Assoc., 1993.

Scofield, C. I., (ed). The new scofield reference bible. Oxford: Oxford Press, 1967.

Shapiro, Ester R. Grief as a family process. New York: The Guilford Press, 1994.

Wolfelt, Alan D. Healing the adult child's grieving heart. Fort Collins, Colorado,: Companion Press, 2002.

Lightning Source UK Ltd.
Milton Keynes UK
UKHW01n1845090818
327018UK00002B/8/P